INTERESTING FACTS

CURIOUS CATS

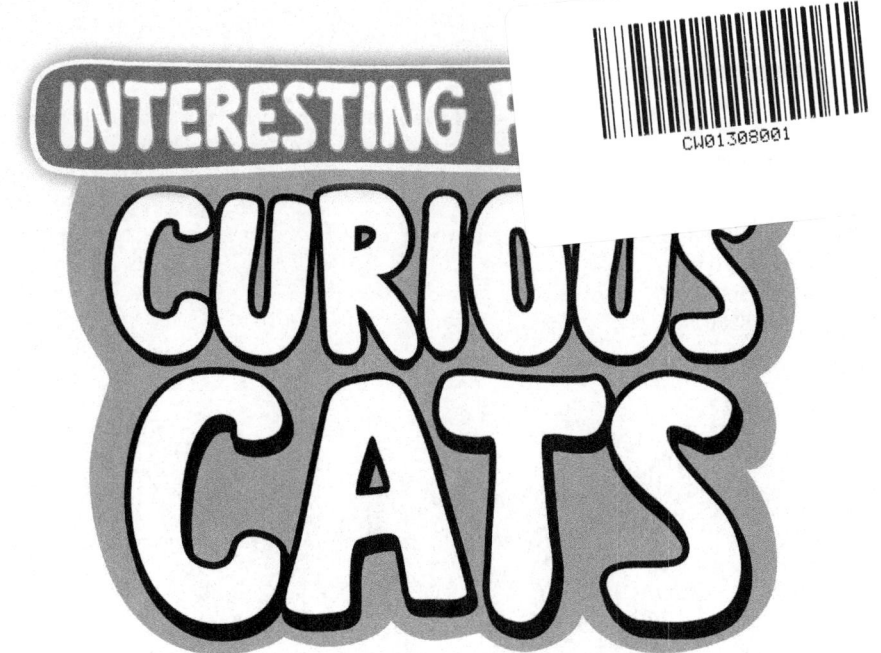

BY

DANIEL KANE

COPYRIGHT © 2023 HHF Press
www.HHFPress.com

COPYRIGHT © 2023 HHF Press
First published 2023

All rights reserved. No part of this book may be reproduced in any form or by any electronic or mechanical means, including information storage and retrieval systems, without permission in writing from the publisher, except by reviewers, who may quote brief passages in a review.

Published in the United States of America by HHF Press
www.HHFPress.com
30 N Gould St Ste 21710
Sheridan, WY 82801

Disclaimer:

All content herein represents the author's own experiences and opinions, and do not represent medical or health advice. The responsibility for the consequences of your actions, including your use or misuse of any suggestion or procedure described in this book lies not with the authors, publisher or distributors of this book. The author or the publisher does not assume any liability for the use of or inability to use any or all of the information contained in this book, nor does the author or publisher accept responsibility for any type of loss or damage that may be experienced by the user as the result of activities occurring from the use of any information in this book. Use the information responsibly and at your own risk.
The author reserves the right to make changes he or she deems required to future versions of the publication to maintain accuracy.

TABLE OF CONTENTS

INTRODUCTION 6
SOME CATNIP BEFORE THE MAIN MEAL: 7
PERPLEXING CAT BEHAVIOR 9
THE RISE OF CAT CULTURE 10
STRANGE BEHAVIORS THAT CATS CONSIDER NORMAL 12
FAMOUS CATS THROUGH HISTORY 14
CAT SUPERSTITIONS FROM AROUND THE WORLD 17
WEIRDEST CONSPIRACY THEORIES ABOUT CATS 19
FAMOUS CRAZY CAT LADIES (AND GENTLEMEN) 20
PERSONALITIES WHO DISLIKE CATS 21
HOW DID CATS GET HERE? 22
AMAZING FELINE ANATOMY 23
WHAT CATS CAN DO THAT HUMANS CAN'T 24
SENSES AND INSTINCTS 25
DOMESTIC CATS IN ANCIENT CIVILIZATIONS 27
THE DEVELOPMENT OF MODERN BREEDS 28
FUNNY CAT EXPRESSIONS 30
THINGS NAMED AFTER CATS 33
CATS LOVE US EVEN THOUGH THEY DON'T LIKE TO SHOW IT 34
CATS ARE GOOD FOR YOU 36
CATS THAT SAVED LIVES 36
UNUSUAL BREEDS 38
WILD FACTS ABOUT WILD CATS 40
HYBRID BREEDS: HALF-CAT, HALF CHOCOLATE? 41
FELINE GENIUSES 43
CATS KNOW THINGS BEFORE YOU DO 44
MEMORY AND EMOTION 45
DO YOU CHOOSE A CAT, OR DOES A CAT CHOOSE YOU? 46

CAT HOUSES (NO, NOT THAT KIND!)	47
DID MY CAT JUST MANIPULATE ME?	48
UNDERSTANDING FELINE BODY LANGUAGE	49
TAIL SIGNALS	50
TRANSLATING CAT SOUNDS	51
CATS CAN TALK WITH OTHER SPECIES	53
PLAY TIME	54
FELINE OLYMPICS	56
CATS THAT ARE FAMOUS FOR HOLDING WORLD RECORDS	57
CAT SHOWS AND COMPETITIONS	59
OUTDOOR ADVENTURES WITH CATS	60
TOYS FOR CATS (OR FOR HUMANS?)	61
WORLD'S WEIRDEST CAT PRODUCTS	62
GAMES AND ACTIVITIES FOR CAT AND "OWNER"	64
CLASSIC CAT BOOKS AND STORIES	65
TALENTED CATS	66
POPULAR CAT FILMS AND TV SHOWS	68
ONLINE AND SOCIAL MEDIA CATS	69
FAMOUS HOLLYWOOD CATS	70
CARTOON CATS	72
RICHEST CATS IN THE WORLD	74
CAT FOOD SURPRISE	75
CAT-FRIENDLY BAKERIES	76
FELINE FASHION AND STYLE	77
CAT-FRIENDLY DESTINATIONS	78
CAT ADVENTURERS	79
SUPERSTITIONS AND FOLKLORE	80
MYSTERIOUS BREEDS AND PHENOMENA	81
PERPLEXING CAT PERSONALITY TRAITS	82
CATS AROUND THE WORLD	83
THREATS TO WILD CAT POPULATIONS	83

PROTECTING OUR FELINE FRIENDS	84
MY THERAPIST IS A CAT	86
CAT JOBS	87
FELINE HEALTH IS UNIQUE	89
DO YOU LOVE YOUR CAT? THEN DO THIS:	90
CAT ADOPTION STORIES	91
AWWWW...	92
HOME IS WHERE THE CAT IS	94
WHY DID MY CAT SPRAY MY CHAIR?	96
MOST COMMON CAT NAMES	97
SOME FUN CAT NAMES	98
CAT-RELATED HOLIDAYS AND FESTIVALS	99
CAT HOLIDAYS, CAT FOODS	101
CAT-RELATED CHARITY EVENTS	102
CAT BURGLARS	103
REAL CATS THAT WERE THIEVES	105
COLORS AND PATTERNS	107
MORE CAT EXPRESSIONS	108
CAT PROPORTIONS	110
INDICATIONS THERE'S A CAT AROUND SOMEWHERE	111
CAT LYRICS	112
CAT'S PAJAMAS	114
CAT LIVES MATTER	115
CRAZY CAT PRODUCTS THAT FAILED	117
AND THE CAT CAME BACK...	118
PROOF THAT CATS HAVE 9 LIVES	119
CATS UNDERSTAND MORE THAN WE THINK	121
TRADITIONAL CAT LIMERICKS	122
MORE RANDOM FACTS THAT DIDN'T MAKE THE CUT, BUT CAN STILL MAKE YOU SMILE	124
THE END... OR IS IT?	129

INTRODUCTION

Meow-there, cat lovers! It's time to let your love for felines run wild as we dive into a world of pawsome trivia about these enigmatic creatures. From the ancient Egyptians to your grandmother's lap, cats have been a part of human history for millennia, and it's high time we give them the recognition they deserve.

Imagine this: you're snuggled up on the couch, surrounded by your favorite furballs, when suddenly a question strikes you. What's the secret behind catnip? How do cats always seem to land on their feet? And why do they knead with their paws? Fear not, my friend, because this book has all the answers you seek and more!

We'll take a deep dive into the wild world of cats, exploring their history, anatomy, and behavior. From the majestic big cats of the African savanna to the tiny tigers in your living room, we'll cover it all. We'll delve into the various breeds of cats, from Siamese to Sphinx, and discover what makes each one so unique. We'll also unravel the many myths and legends surrounding cats, from black cats being bad luck to the origin of the idea that they have nine lives.

But this book isn't just about facts, it's about fun! We'll take a walk on the wild side as we explore the wacky and wonderful world of cat memes, videos, and merchandise. We'll meet famous felines from history, from Cleopatra's pampered pets to the internet-famous Grumpy Cat. And we'll see how cats have made their mark on pop culture, from literature to television to music.

So grab a bowl of catnip and get comfortable, because we're about to embark on a journey through the feline universe like no other. With whiskers twitching with excitement, this book is perfect for cat lovers of all ages, whether you're a seasoned pro or a curious observer. The cat's out of the bag, and it's time to explore the amazing world of cat trivia!

SOME CATNIP BEFORE THE MAIN MEAL:

- ❖ Catnip can produce a similar effect to LSD or marijuana in cats, with the effects of the chemical nepetalactone wearing off after 15 minutes.
- ❖ Cats have a unique gait, walking like camels and giraffes by moving both of their right feet first, followed by both of their left feet.
- ❖ The oldest cat video dates back to 1894 and is called "Boxing Cats."
- ❖ Cats share an impressive 95.6% of their genome with tigers, exhibiting similar behaviors such as scratching to mark their territory and playing with prey.
- ❖ With a highly developed brain, cats have nearly twice as many neurons in their cerebral cortex as dogs, allowing for advanced problem-solving and hunting skills. That explains a lot!
- ❖ Unlike other mammals, cats have a unique genetic makeup that prevents them from tasting sweetness.
- ❖ Cats have a different visual acuity compared to humans, with poor close-up vision but exceptional peripheral and night vision.
- ❖ Cats may perceive slow-moving objects as stagnant and have difficulty tracking their motion.
- ❖ With 18 toes in total, cats have five toes on each front paw and four toes on each back paw, providing extra grip and agility. Polydactyl cats have more than 18 toes and are a rare genetic variation.
- ❖ Some cats have a fondness for water and can swim.

- Cats are such fast sprinters that a house cat could beat superstar runner Usain Bolt in the 200 meter dash.
- Cats can exhibit strong food preferences and may refuse unpalatable food to the point of starvation.
- Cats are known for their impressive jumping abilities, able to leap up to six times their own body length in a single bound.
- Due to the downward curving of their claws, cats are unable to climb down trees head-first and must reverse their descent.
- With a unique skeletal structure, cats have floating collarbones and a total of 230 bones in their bodies. This is one of the reasons they always land on their feet.
- Cats have a specialized organ, the Jacobson's organ, which allows them to detect scents in the air and determine their surroundings.
- In addition to whiskers on their faces, cats also have whiskers on the backs of their front legs, providing them with additional sensory information.
- Among all mammals, cats have the largest eyes relative to the size of their heads, providing them with exceptional vision in low light conditions.
- Cats have adapted to be stealthy hunters, with soft paw pads that allow them to walk silently and rough tongues that can lick bones clean of any meat.
- A cat with a question-mark-shaped tail is asking, "Want to play?"
- Cats use their tails for balance and their whiskers to determine if small spaces are safe to enter, with their whiskers being about the same width as their bodies.
- 40% of cats have a preference for either their left or right paw, with some cats being ambidextrous. Studies have shown that male cats are more likely to be left-pawed, while female cats tend to favor using their right paws.
- Grooming is an important part of a cat's routine, taking up to a third of their waking hours. It helps stimulate blood flow, regulate body temperature, and promote relaxation for cats.
- Cats may yawn as a way to end a confrontation with another animal. Think of it as their "talk to the hand" gesture.

- The average lifespan of cats increased by a year between 2002 and 2012.
- Indoor cats tend to have longer lifespans than outdoor cats.
- Purring may serve as a self-soothing mechanism for cats, occurring both in happy and stressful situations.
- Many cats are lactose intolerant and should not be given dairy products.
- Female cats can become pregnant as early as 4 months of age.
- Grapes, raisins, onions, garlic, and chives are toxic to cats and can cause serious health problems.
- Want your cat to sleep at night? Feed it a substantial evening meal.
- Cats have up to 100 different vocalizations — dogs only have 10.
- Fixed male cats require fewer calories to maintain their weight and neutering or spaying can increase a cat's lifespan by up to 62% for males and 39% for females.

PERPLEXING CAT BEHAVIOR

- Cats may squint or wink to signal relaxation and trust, as they feel comfortable enough to let their guard down around you.
- When a cat yawns in your presence, it could be a sign of trust and comfort, as they feel safe enough to engage in this vulnerable behavior.
- The unique "M" marking on the forehead of tabby cats is not just a physical trait; it's believed to be an indicator of a friendly and sociable personality.
- Cats scratch not only to sharpen their claws but also to communicate, as it leaves both a visual marker and a scent from their paw pads to claim territory.
- Gentle nibbling or nipping from your cat can be a sign of affection, as they may be engaging in mutual grooming behavior, similar to how they would with another cat.
- Cats might chirp or chatter at insects, just as they do with birds or other prey, as an expression of excitement or anticipation.
- An S-shaped tail can be a sign of excitement or playfulness, indicating that your cat may be in a particularly frisky mood.

- Cats might dig excessively in their litter boxes to mark their territory or as a displacement behavior when they are feeling stressed or anxious.
- Cats may flick their tongues rapidly when they are annoyed or irritated, as it can be a sign of frustration or a warning to back off.
- Cats often practice their pouncing skills on toys or even their human's feet, honing their hunting instincts in a safe environment.
- A cat's whiskers might vibrate rapidly when they are excited, alert, or focused on an object of interest, such as a toy or a treat.

THE RISE OF CAT CULTURE

- The ancient Egyptians not only revered cats as sacred animals, but they also had a festival in honor of the cat goddess, Bastet. This annual event included music, dancing, and the consumption of large amounts of wine.
- Cats faced a tough time during the Middle Ages in Europe, as they were often associated with witchcraft and superstition. However, their popularity rebounded due to their pest control abilities during the Black Death, which decimated the rat population.
- Cats have been featured in numerous literary works throughout history. One famous example is "The Cat and the Mouse in Partnership," a German fairy tale from the Brothers Grimm collection.

- Cats have also graced the stage, most notably in the long-running musical "Cats" by Andrew Lloyd Webber. The show is based on T.S. Eliot's poetry collection "Old Possum's Book of Practical Cats."
- The character Puss in Boots, a cunning and resourceful cat, has been a beloved figure in European folklore since the 16th century. The story has been adapted into various forms, including an animated film featuring the voice of Antonio Banderas.
- The iconic Japanese character Hello Kitty, created by Yuko Shimizu in 1974, has become a global phenomenon. Despite being a cat, she is portrayed without a mouth to symbolize the universality of emotions.
- Cats have been a popular subject in art for centuries, appearing in the works of artists like Leonardo da Vinci, Pablo Picasso, and Henri Matisse.
- Cat motifs have made their way into the world of fashion, with designers like Dolce & Gabbana, Gucci, and Stella McCartney featuring feline-inspired designs in their collections.
- World Cat Day, celebrated on August 8th, is an international event that promotes the love and appreciation of cats. The day encourages the adoption of cats from shelters and raises awareness about feline welfare issues.
- In the 19th century, cat shows became popular in England and helped to establish the modern-day breeds of cats.
- In the late 1800s, the development of cat litter made it more practical to keep cats as indoor pets.
- The Siamese cat was one of the first breeds of cats to be imported to the Western world and quickly became popular due to its unique appearance and social personality. They were considered a symbol of luxury and were often owned by royalty.
- The first cat-themed comic strip, "Katzenjammer Kids," was created in 1897 and has since been followed by many others, cementing cats' place in popular culture.
- The idea of cat ladies, or women who live with many cats, has been around for centuries, but in recent years has become a more accepted and celebrated lifestyle.

STRANGE BEHAVIORS THAT CATS CONSIDER NORMAL

- ❖ The "blep" is a hilarious cat quirk where they forget to retract their tongues, often resulting in an amusing and endearing expression. It's a charming display of feline derpiness.
- ❖ Some cats defy their species' reputation for water aversion by enjoying water play, splashing in sinks or bathtubs. These feline mermaids may even swim in shallow water!
- ❖ Cats may exhibit the peculiar habit of "head pressing" against walls or furniture. While it might look quirky, it can signal neurological issues and warrants a vet consultation.
- ❖ If you've witnessed a cat "chattering," you've seen them mimic bird noises. This strange behavior is likely linked to their predatory instincts, practicing hunting their feathered friends.
- ❖ Cats occasionally bring "gifts" like dead mice or birds, which is their way of showing affection and demonstrating their teaching abilities. It's a gruesome yet oddly touching gesture of love.
- ❖ Some cats have an obsessive behavior of compulsively licking plastic bags. This puzzling fixation may be due to the taste, texture, or scent of the plastic. Shopping bag connoisseurs, perhaps?

- When cats exhibit a "slow blink," it's a sign of trust and relaxation. By closing their eyes in your presence, they're communicating that they feel safe and comfortable around you.
- Cats occasionally nibble on grass or plants. This odd behavior helps them with digestion and hairball expulsion. Who would've guessed our carnivorous friends craved the occasional salad?
- A cat's "air kneading" involves making kneading motions without touching anything. It's as if they're sculpting invisible clay masterpieces or performing a peculiar feline ballet.
- Cats sometimes practice "shadow boxing," swatting at nonexistent prey in mid-air. Are they honing their reflexes and hunting skills, or training for a secret underground cat fight club?
- Cats engaging in "tail chasing" could be due to pent-up energy, curiosity, or playfulness. This behavior is more common in kittens, but adult cats may continue the habit, providing an entertaining display for their owners.
- When cats practice "bunting," they're leaving their scent on objects or people. This is a form of communication, allowing them to establish their presence and create a familiar environment with their scent markers.
- Cats knocking items off surfaces might be an attempt to gain attention or a form of play. This behavior can also be a result of their hunting instincts, as they explore their environment and interact with various objects.
- The "flehmen response", characteristic lip-curling expression, allows cats to draw scent molecules into their vomeronasal organ, a specialized scent-analyzing structure in the roof of their mouth. This behavior helps them better understand their surroundings.
- "Trilling" is a unique sound some cats use to communicate with their owners or other cats. It often signifies contentment, excitement, or a desire for interaction, making it a versatile and expressive form of feline communication.
- "Zoomies," or sudden bursts of energy, are common in cats as a way to release pent-up energy or engage in play. These episodes can also be a manifestation of their hunting instincts, as they race and pounce around the house.

- Cats "stalking" their humans or other animals is a manifestation of their natural predatory instincts. This behavior allows them to practice and hone their hunting skills, even in domesticated settings.
- The "butt wiggle" exhibited by cats before pouncing helps them establish balance, ensuring a solid foundation for the leap. This behavior enables them to focus and accurately gauge the distance to their target.
- Cats may watch television or computer screens because they're attracted to the movement, colors, and sounds. This form of visual stimulation can be engaging and entertaining for cats, especially when depicting prey-like objects.
- Cats developing an attachment to a specific toy or object may be a source of comfort or security for them. These objects often hold their scent, which can help create a familiar and reassuring environment for the cat.

FAMOUS CATS THROUGH HISTORY

- Félicette, a French feline, became the first and only cat astronaut in 1963. She completed a successful 15-minute suborbital flight and was safely recovered afterward.
- Unsinkable Sam, a black and white cat, miraculously survived the sinking of three separate ships during World War II. He was rescued from the wreckage each time, earning his extraordinary nickname.

- Socks, a tuxedo cat, was the "First Cat" of the United States during Bill Clinton's presidency. He captured the hearts of the nation and even inspired a children's book.
- CC, or Copy Cat, was the world's first cloned cat, born in 2001. This scientific breakthrough raised ethical questions and highlighted the possibilities of genetic replication in animals.
- Hamish McHamish, a Scottish ginger cat, gained local fame in St Andrews for his sociable nature. He even had a bronze statue erected in his honor after his death in 2014.
- Tama, a calico cat, served as the stationmaster for Kishi Station in Japan. Her appointment in 2007 helped save the struggling railway line and turned her into a beloved tourist attraction.
- Hodge, the beloved pet of Samuel Johnson, the 18th-century English writer, was immortalized in a bronze statue in London. The statue shows Hodge sitting on a dictionary, honoring their unique bond.
- Dewey Readmore Books, a library cat in Spencer, Iowa, brought joy to the community for 19 years. His life story inspired the best-selling book, "Dewey: The Small-Town Library Cat Who Touched the World."
- Larry, a rescue cat, has served as the "Chief Mouser" at the British Prime Minister's residence, 10 Downing Street, since 2011. He's an important part of the UK's political landscape.
- Able Seacat Simon, a ship's cat on the HMS Amethyst, became a hero in 1949 during the Yangtze Incident. He received the Dickin Medal, the animal equivalent of the Victoria Cross, for his bravery and rat-catching prowess.
- Choupette Lagerfeld, the pampered Birman cat, was the beloved pet of fashion icon Karl Lagerfeld. She enjoyed a luxurious life, had personal maids, and even inspired a fashion line.
- Tommaso, an Italian stray cat, inherited a staggering $13 million estate from his owner, Maria Assunta, in 2011. He went from rags to riches overnight, becoming one of the wealthiest pets in history.
- Blackie, the Guinness World Record holder for the world's wealthiest cat, inherited a $12.5 million fortune when his British owner, Ben Rea, passed away in 1988.

- Tibs the Great, a 23-pound feline, served as the official "Chief Mouser" for the General Post Office headquarters in London from 1950 to 1964, becoming a celebrated postal hero.

- Fred the Undercover Cat, a domestic shorthair, assisted the NYPD in a sting operation in 2006. He posed as a sick cat, helping to apprehend a man selling sick animals without a license.

- Peter, the Lord's cat, was a celebrated feline at the Lord's Cricket Ground in London. He lived there for 12 years, becoming a fixture at the grounds and even having an obituary published in Wisden Cricketers' Almanack.

- Nala, a globetrotting adventure cat, accompanied her owner, Dean Nicholson, on a bicycle journey across Europe. Their story went viral, and they now use their fame to raise awareness for animal rescue organizations.

- Cairo, a Navy SEAL K-9 dog, helped take down Osama bin Laden. In the aftermath, the CIA revealed that they had once used cats in a covert operation known as "Acoustic Kitty" in the 1960s, which was eventually deemed a failure.

- Baidian'er, a stray cat living at Beijing's Palace Museum, gained internet fame for accurately "predicting" the outcomes of 2018 World Cup matches by choosing between food bowls representing competing teams.

- Stubbs, a ginger cat, served as the honorary mayor of Talkeetna, Alaska, for 20 years. The feline's unique political position garnered international attention and made him a beloved figure in the town.

- Professor Powel, a British cat, became famous in the early 20th century for his ability to perform complex mathematical calculations, earning him the title of "The Cat Who Could Do Sums."

- Venus, the Two-Faced Cat, became famous in 2009 for her unique appearance, which features two different colored eyes and two distinct facial expressions.

- Henri, le Chat Noir, a black-and-white tuxedo cat from the United States, became famous in the early 2000s for his philosophical musings and sarcastic commentary, which have been widely shared on social media.

CAT SUPERSTITIONS FROM AROUND THE WORLD

- ❖ In Japan, the "Maneki Neko" or "beckoning cat" is a popular talisman believed to bring good fortune. These cat figurines, often found in businesses, are thought to attract wealth and prosperity.
- ❖ In ancient Egypt, it was believed that a cat's gaze held protective powers. Egyptians placed statues of cats with their eyes wide open to ward off evil spirits.
- ❖ Sailors in the British Isles considered black cats to be good luck charms. They believed that having one onboard would ensure a safe and prosperous voyage.
- ❖ In Lithuanian folklore, it's said that if a cat jumps over a deceased person's body, the deceased will become a vampire. To prevent this, the cat must be driven away or killed.
- ❖ In parts of the United Kingdom, it was once believed that stroking a black cat's tail could cure a sty in the eye. The healing powers of feline fur seem to know no bounds!
- ❖ In some Native American tribes, it's thought that dreaming of a cat signals treachery or deception. Those who experience such dreams are advised to be cautious in their dealings.
- ❖ In ancient Rome, cats were considered symbols of liberty. They roamed the streets freely and were even allowed to enter the sacred temples of the goddess Diana.

- In Norse mythology, the goddess Freyja was said to travel in a chariot pulled by two powerful cats. These feline companions symbolized fertility and abundance, key aspects of the goddess's domain.

- In medieval Europe, some people believed that witches could shape-shift into cats. This superstition led to the persecution of both witches and cats during times of unrest.

- In Malaysia, a widely held superstition suggests that if you step on a cat's tail, you'll experience bad luck in love. The only remedy is to wait for the cat to forgive you and move on.

- In parts of Eastern Europe, it's believed that if a cat cleans its face and paws near the front door, a visitor will soon arrive. This superstition may have arisen from the cat's keen senses detecting approaching guests.

- In early American folklore, it was thought that if a cat slept with its back to the fire, it was a sign of cold weather or a storm approaching. Cats were thought to be sensitive to changes in atmospheric pressure.

- In Scotland, it's said that a stray black cat appearing on your doorstep is a sign of good fortune. However, if the cat leaves, so does the luck, so it's best to keep the feline visitor around!

- In ancient Persia, cats were believed to have mystical powers and were often depicted with wings. These mythical winged cats were thought to protect people from evil spirits and misfortune.

- In Italian folklore, it's believed that if a cat sneezes, the entire household will experience good luck. The sneeze is thought to chase away negative energy and usher in a wave of positivity.

- While various cultures have different beliefs and remedies for a black cat crossing your path, one common antidote is to take a few steps backward and then walk around the area where the cat crossed. This action is thought to reverse the perceived bad luck. Another approach is to wait for someone else to pass the same path before continuing, effectively passing the bad luck to them. However, it's essential to remember that these superstitions are not based on factual evidence, and black cats are simply ordinary animals with no inherent power to bring good or bad luck :)

WEIRDEST CONSPIRACY THEORIES ABOUT CATS

- The "Cats are aliens" theory suggests that cats are actually extraterrestrial beings that were sent to Earth to observe humans and report back to their home planet.
- The "Cat conspiracy to take over the world" theory proposes that cats are secretly plotting to overthrow humanity and establish themselves as the dominant species on the planet.
- The "Cats are spies" theory suggests that cats are actually being used as spies by governments and intelligence agencies to gather information on citizens.
- The "Cat Illuminati" theory suggests that a secret society of cats exists, manipulating world events and controlling human behavior from behind the scenes.
- The "Catnip conspiracy" theory proposes that the popularity of catnip among cats is actually part of a grand scheme to keep cats docile and prevent them from rebelling against their human overlords.
- The "Cat telepathy" theory suggests that cats are able to communicate telepathically with each other and with humans, allowing them to share information and coordinate their actions.
- The "Cat mind control" theory proposes that cats possess the ability to control human minds, manipulating them into doing their bidding.
- The "Cat language" theory suggests that cats have their own unique language that is understood only by other cats, and that humans are unable to comprehend it.
- The "Cat weather control" theory proposes that cats are able to control the weather using their purring and other mysterious methods.
- The "Cat reincarnation" theory suggests that cats are able to reincarnate themselves after they die, allowing them to live multiple lives and continue their work in furthering their secret agenda.
- The Catacomb Cats of Paris are said to live in the underground catacombs beneath the city, guarding the bones of the dead and adding to the eerie atmosphere of the historic site.
- Aoshima Island, Japan, is said to be home to a large population of feral cats and is rumored to be a portal to another dimension, making it a mysterious and intriguing location.

FAMOUS CRAZY CAT LADIES (AND GENTLEMEN)

- Andy Warhol, the famous pop artist, was known for his love of cats. He shared his New York City townhouse with a large number of feline companions. At one point, he had as many as 25 cats, almost all of which were named Sam, except for one named Hester.
- Eleanor Roosevelt, the First Lady of the United States, was known to have numerous cats in the White House during her husband Franklin D. Roosevelt's presidency, including a favorite named Smoky.
- Vivien Leigh, the famous actress who starred in "Gone with the Wind," was a devoted cat lover. At one point, she had 15 cats living in her home, which she affectionately referred to as her "family."
- Edith Wharton, the Pulitzer Prize-winning author, was an avid cat lover. Her home was filled with feline companions, and she even had a pet cemetery on her property to bury her beloved cats.
- Freddie Mercury, the lead vocalist of Queen, was a self-proclaimed cat lady. He owned numerous cats throughout his life and even dedicated his solo album "Mr. Bad Guy" to his cats, Jerry, Tom, Oscar, and Tiffany.
- Jean Cocteau, a French poet and filmmaker, was known for his love of cats. He had many cats in his home and even wrote a book called "La Chat et la Bicyclette," which centered on a cat named Madeline.
- Ernest Hemingway, the celebrated American author, had a passion for cats. His home in Key West, Florida, was filled with cats, many of which

were polydactyl (having extra toes). Today, the Ernest Hemingway Home and Museum is a sanctuary for the descendants of his cats.

- ❖ Mark Twain, the renowned American author, was known for his love of cats. At one point, he had up to 19 cats in his home. He would rent cats from neighbors when he was traveling, as he believed cats brought him comfort and inspiration.
- ❖ Josephine Bonaparte, wife of Napoleon Bonaparte, was an avid cat lover. She was known to have numerous cats in her home, Château de Malmaison, and treated them as treasured companions.
- ❖ Kate Benjamin, a cat expert, and the founder of the cat-themed design company Hauspanther, is a modern-day cat lady. She shares her home with more than a dozen cats, turning it into a cat-friendly paradise filled with cat climbing walls, furniture, and unique cat toys.

PERSONALITIES WHO DISLIKE CATS

- ❖ Tom Hardy: The actor has said that he is a cat hater and prefers dogs as pets, joking in an interview that he thinks cats are "snobbish."
- ❖ Simon Cowell: The music executive and television personality has expressed his dislike of cats in several interviews and once famously said, "I'm allergic to cats and I'm allergic to talent."
- ❖ Louis C.K.: The comedian has expressed his dislike of cats in several stand-up routines, including one in which he jokes that cats are "like girls, only they have fur."
- ❖ Miley Cyrus: The singer and actress is a cat lover, but has also expressed her fear of cats due to their unpredictability and tendency to scratch.
- ❖ Vladimir Putin: The Russian President has expressed his dislike of cats in several interviews and once famously said, "I'm a dog man, not a cat man."
- ❖ Ben Stiller: The actor has said that he is allergic to cats and cannot be around them for long periods of time, joking in an interview that he is "allergic to being scratched."
- ❖ Woody Allen: The filmmaker has expressed his dislike of cats in interviews and even wrote a short story called "The Abominable Snowman" about a cat that he hated.

- Michael Bloomberg: The former New York City mayor is known to be a cat hater and has been quoted as saying, "I don't like cats. I don't like dogs. I don't like animals."
- Winston Churchill: The former British Prime Minister reportedly once said, "I like pigs. Dogs look up to us. Cats look down on us. Pigs treat us as equals."
- Napoleon Bonaparte: The French Emperor was said to despise cats and believed that they were a symbol of superstition.
- Steve Jobs: The late Apple co-founder was known to be a cat hater and even reportedly had a "no cats allowed" policy at his company's headquarters.
- James Patterson: The best-selling author has expressed his dislike of cats in interviews and has even written a book called "The Cat Who Blew the Whistle," in which the main character dislikes cats.

HOW DID CATS GET HERE?

- The earliest ancestors of domestic cats were likely small wild cats that lived in the Near East and Africa about 10 million years ago.
- Domestic cats are descendants of the African wildcat, Felis silvestris lybica, and are not closely related to other wildcat species.
- The domestication of cats likely occurred around 7500 BCE, when humans began to settle down and store grain, attracting mice and other pests.
- The domestication of cats was a gradual process, with wildcats gradually becoming more tolerant of human presence and eventually evolving into domestic cats.
- Domestication was not intentional, as humans initially kept cats around to control pests. Over time, however, cats became valued for their companionship and hunting abilities.
- Domestic cats are not fully domesticated, as they still retain many of their wild instincts and behaviors.
- Despite their domestication, today's cats have not evolved significantly from their wild ancestors, as selective breeding has only emphasized certain physical traits.

- Domestic cats are capable of interbreeding with wildcats, and there are populations of feral cats that are descendants of domesticated cats that have returned to the wild.
- Cats are one of the most widespread domestic animals in the world, and are found on every continent except Antarctica.
- Cats are not native to the Americas, and were likely brought over by European settlers during the colonial era.

AMAZING FELINE ANATOMY

- The pads on a cat's paws are covered in a thick layer of fat that provides insulation and shock absorption, allowing them to walk quietly and land softly.
- Cats have a flexible spine and extremely strong hind legs, allowing them to jump up to six times their body length in a single leap.
- Cats have a unique flexible skeletal structure, with more than two dozen bones in their spine that allow them to contort and twist in ways that would break human bones.
- Cats have a highly specialized digestive system that is optimized for breaking down animal protein, and they are unable to properly digest plant-based protein sources.

- Cats have an incredibly efficient kidney system that is capable of filtering impurities from their bloodstream and conserving water, even in times of dehydration.
- Cats have a highly sensitive sense of smell, with a scent gland in their mouth that allows them to leave scent marks on objects and surfaces.
- Cats have a flexible and retractable set of claws, which they use for hunting and climbing, and can retract them when not in use to keep them sharp.
- Cats have a specialized inner ear structure that allows them to detect even the slightest sounds and movements, making them excellent hunters.
- The fur of a cat is covered in tiny hooks called spines, which trap loose fur and help keep the coat clean and in good condition.
- Cats have a unique muscle structure in their eyes that allows them to quickly change the shape of their eyes to focus on objects at different distances, giving them exceptional depth perception.
- Cats have a highly sensitive and flexible tail, which they use to balance themselves and communicate with other cats.
- Cats have a specialized set of teeth, including long and sharp canines, that are adapted for hunting and killing prey.
- Cats have a specialized membrane in their ears called the pinna, which can move independently in any direction and amplify sounds, allowing them to detect even the slightest noises.
- Cats have a specialized nervous system that allows them to recover quickly from falls and injuries, and also helps them stay calm and relaxed in stressful situations.

WHAT CATS CAN DO THAT HUMANS CAN'T

- Cats can rotate their ears up to 180 degrees, allowing them to locate sounds with incredible precision.
- Cats can jump up to six times their own body length, thanks to their powerful leg muscles and flexible spines.
- Cats have a special organ in their mouth called the Jacobson's organ, which allows them to taste and smell things that humans can't.

- Cats have retractable claws, which they can extend and retract at will, giving them better traction and grip than humans.
- Cats are able to see in almost complete darkness due to their highly sensitive eyes and special reflective layer behind their retina.
- Cats are excellent hunters and have the ability to catch prey with their teeth and claws in just a fraction of a second.
- Cats have the ability to self-groom using their rough tongues, which have tiny hooks that help remove dirt and loose fur from their coat.
- Cats have a highly developed sense of balance and can walk along narrow surfaces or climb trees with ease.
- Cats have a natural instinct to hide when they feel threatened or scared, using their stealth and agility to escape danger.
- Cats are able to sleep for up to 16 hours a day, which is essential for their overall health and well-being.

SENSES AND INSTINCTS

- Cats' whiskers are not just for show; they serve as essential sensory organs. Whiskers can detect even the slightest changes in air currents, helping cats navigate in darkness and avoid obstacles.
- Cats have extraordinary night vision due to the higher number of rod cells in their eyes compared to humans. They can see light at levels six

times lower than humans, giving them a significant advantage when hunting in low light.

- ❖ Cats have an incredible sense of hearing, capable of detecting sounds as high as 64 kHz (compared to humans, who can only hear up to 20 kHz). This heightened sense helps cats locate prey and avoid predators.
- ❖ Cats have a special organ called the Jacobson's organ, located on the roof of their mouth. When they make a funny face, opening their mouth and curling their upper lip, they are using the Flehmen response to better analyze scents.
- ❖ Cats' purring is not only a sign of contentment; it also serves as a form of self-healing. The frequency of a cat's purr (around 25-150 Hz) has been found to promote bone density, tissue healing, and pain relief.
- ❖ A cat's tail can reveal a lot about its mood. A raised tail typically indicates happiness, while a puffed-up tail signals fear or aggression. A twitching tail may mean a cat is irritated or concentrating on prey.
- ❖ Cats have special whiskers above their eyes, known as supraorbital whiskers, which help them detect objects in their environment, protect their eyes from debris, and navigate difficult terrain.
- ❖ Cats have powerful hind legs, which allow them to make impressive vertical leaps. They can jump up to six times their body length in a single bound, giving them a significant advantage when chasing prey or avoiding danger.
- ❖ Cats have an innate ability to land on their feet after a fall, thanks to their "righting reflex." They can quickly twist their flexible spine and use their tail for balance, ensuring a safe landing.
- ❖ Cats have scent glands in their cheeks, chin, and forehead, which they use to mark their territory. By rubbing their face on objects or people, they are leaving behind their scent, claiming ownership, and creating a familiar environment.
- ❖ Cats have a natural instinct to avoid direct eye contact, which is thought to be a way to avoid confrontations with other animals in the wild and communicate submissiveness.
- ❖ Cats have the ability to detect changes in air pressure, which helps them to predict the arrival of storms and other weather patterns.

DOMESTIC CATS IN ANCIENT CIVILIZATIONS

- ❖ Cats were highly revered in ancient Egyptian society. They were considered sacred animals and were often associated with the goddess Bastet, who symbolized protection, fertility, and motherhood.

- ❖ In ancient Egypt, some cats received lavish burials alongside their human owners. These feline mummies were often placed in elaborate sarcophagi and accompanied by offerings to ensure a comfortable afterlife.

- ❖ Killing a cat in ancient Egypt, even accidentally, was considered a severe crime punishable by death. Cats were so important that harming one was seen as an affront to the gods.

- ❖ Cats were so valued in ancient Egypt that there was a strict ban on exporting them to other countries. However, this didn't stop traders from smuggling cats to Greece, Rome, and other parts of the Mediterranean.

- ❖ Cats were introduced to the Roman Empire through trade with Egypt. The Romans appreciated cats for their pest control abilities and often kept them on ships and in granaries to protect valuable goods from rodents.

- ❖ In Norse mythology, the goddess Freyja, who represented love, fertility, and beauty, was often depicted riding a chariot pulled by two large cats. These cats were said to be a gift from the god Thor.

- In ancient China, cats were admired for their hunting skills and gracefulness. They were often associated with the goddess Li Shou, who was believed to protect crops from pests like rats and locusts.
- Cats were held in high esteem in Islamic culture, and there are several stories about their kindness and companionship with the Prophet Muhammad. He is said to have loved cats and often let them rest on his lap.
- The Maneki Neko, or "beckoning cat," is a popular symbol of good luck and prosperity in Japan. It is believed to have originated in the Edo period (1603-1868) and is often displayed in shops and businesses to attract customers.
- Cats were not as commonly mentioned in ancient Indian texts, but there is evidence of domesticated cats in the Indian subcontinent dating back to around 2000 BCE. They were likely used for pest control in agricultural communities and later became integrated into Indian society as companion animals.

THE DEVELOPMENT OF MODERN BREEDS

- Persian cats were first brought to Europe from Persia (modern-day Iran) in the 1600s by traders and diplomats. Their luxurious, long-haired coats and gentle temperament made them a favorite among European aristocracy.

- The domestication of cats can be traced back to around 7500 BCE, with the African wildcat (Felis silvestris lybica) as their most likely ancestor. These wildcats were attracted to human settlements due to abundant food sources like rodents.

- Initially, domesticated cats evolved naturally, with various coat colors and patterns emerging over time. Different environments and selective breeding by humans further diversified the gene pool, leading to distinct regional characteristics.

- One of the oldest known cat breeds, the Egyptian Mau, can be traced back to ancient Egyptian civilization. Its spotted coat and elegant build are reminiscent of the cats depicted in ancient artwork.

- Originating in Siam (now Thailand), Siamese cats date back to at least the 14th century. The breed's striking appearance, with its blue almond-shaped eyes and color-pointed coat, made it a popular gift among royal and noble families.

- Hailing from the Isle of Man, Manx cats are best known for their unique tailless appearance. This trait likely developed through a natural genetic mutation, which was then encouraged by islanders through selective breeding.

- The Maine Coon is the largest domesticated cat breed and is believed to have originated in North America. Its thick, water-resistant coat and bushy tail are adaptations to the harsh winters of the northeastern United States.

- With their sleek, muscular bodies and short, ticked coats, Abyssinians resemble the African wildcat. Their origins are not well-documented, but they are believed to have originated in Ethiopia or ancient Egypt.

- The Russian Blue cat breed is known for its dense, shimmering blue-grey coat and green eyes. It is believed to have originated in the port city of Arkhangelsk, Russia, and was brought to Europe by sailors in the 1800s.

- Bengal cats are a hybrid breed created by crossing the Asian leopard cat with domestic breeds. Developed in the United States in the 1970s, their distinct leopard-like appearance has made them a popular choice among cat enthusiasts.

- The hairless Sphynx cat was created through selective breeding of cats with a natural genetic mutation. The breed originated in Canada in the 1960s and is known for its unique appearance and friendly, inquisitive nature.

- ❖ The Scottish Fold breed is characterized by its distinctive folded ears, which are the result of a genetic mutation. The first Scottish Fold was discovered on a farm in Scotland in the 1960s, and its descendants were later bred to create the breed we know today.

- ❖ Developed in the United States in the 1960s, Ragdoll cats are known for their docile, affectionate nature and striking blue eyes. They are a large breed with semi-long, silky fur and a color-pointed pattern.

- ❖ The Exotic Shorthair is a breed created by crossing Persian cats with American Shorthairs and other shorthaired breeds. Developed in the United States in the 1960s, they are similar to Persians in temperament and appearance but with a shorter, easier-to-maintain coat.

- ❖ The Toyger is a breed designed to resemble a miniature tiger, with bold, dark stripes on a vivid orange coat. Its name is a portmanteau of the words "toy" and "tiger", and it was created by breeding a Bengal cat with a striped domestic shorthair.

FUNNY CAT EXPRESSIONS

- ❖ "Cat's pajamas" - something that is considered the best or most fashionable. This expression is used to describe something that is highly desirable or fashionable. It is thought to have originated in the 1920s and was used to describe the latest and greatest in fashion or technology.

- ❖ "Cat got your tongue": This expression is used to ask someone why they are not speaking, often when they are expected to. It is thought to have originated from the practice of using a cat-o'-nine-tails whip to extract information from sailors who were captured as prisoners of war. The whip was said to be so painful that it would make even the toughest sailor unable to speak.

- "Let the cat out of the bag": This expression means to reveal a secret or to spoil a surprise. It is thought to have originated from the practice of selling live pigs in bags at markets. If the seller opened the bag to show the pig, it was said to have "let the cat out of the bag." This would reveal the contents of the bag and reduce its value, as the buyer would know exactly what they were getting.

- "Raining cats and dogs": This expression is used to describe heavy rain. The origin of this phrase is unclear, but it may be related to the idea that in olden times, heavy rain was so strong that it could carry small animals like cats and dogs off the ground and into the air. Another theory is that it is a corruption of the phrase "raining it down cats and dogs," which was used to describe heavy rain in England during the 1600s.

- "Cool cat" - a person who is calm and confident. This expression is used to describe someone who is relaxed and in control, even in stressful situations. It is thought to have originated in the 1950s and 1960s and was used to describe someone who was hip and fashionable.

- "Fat cat" - a wealthy person, often used to describe a person who is greedy or corrupt. This expression is used to describe someone who is well-off and perhaps seen as exploiting their wealth or power. It is thought to have originated in the early 1900s and was used to describe wealthy industrialists and business owners.

- "Cat's meow" - something that is considered the best or most attractive. This expression is used to describe something that is highly desirable or fashionable. It is thought to have originated in the early 1900s and was used to describe the latest and greatest in fashion or technology.

- "Play cat and mouse" - to engage in a game or activity that involves trickery or evasion. This expression is used to describe a situation where one person is trying to outwit or outmaneuver another. It is thought to have originated from the idea of a cat playing with a mouse before killing it.

- "Cat nap" - a brief nap or sleep. This expression is used to describe a short, usually daytime, nap. The origin of this phrase is unclear, but it may be related to the idea of a cat taking a quick nap and then being alert and ready to play again.

- "Cat fight" - a verbal or physical altercation between two women. This expression is used to describe a conflict or argument between two women. The origin of this phrase is unclear, but it may be related to the idea of two cats hissing and swatting at each other.

- "The cat's whiskers" - something that is considered the best or most attractive. This expression is used to describe something that is highly desirable or fashionable. It is thought to have originated in the early 1900s and was used to describe the latest and greatest in fashion or technology.

- "Not enough room to swing a cat" - used to describe a small or cramped space. This expression is used to describe a space that is too small or cramped to accommodate even basic activities. It is thought to have originated in the 1700s and was used to describe the cramped conditions on ships, where sailors would be punished by being beaten with a whip known as a cat o' nine tails.

- "Cat on a hot tin roof" - used to describe a person who is restless or agitated. This expression is used to describe a person who is feeling uneasy or unsettled. It is thought to have originated from the play of the same name by Tennessee Williams, in which the main character is described as feeling like a cat on a hot tin roof due to the intense pressure he is under.

- "Fight like cats and dogs" - used to describe two people or groups who are constantly arguing or in conflict. This expression is used to describe a situation where two people or groups are constantly arguing or in conflict. The origin of this phrase is unclear, but it may be related to the idea of two animals who are natural enemies, such as cats and dogs, constantly fighting.

- "Copycat" - a person who imitates or copies someone else. This expression is used to describe a person who imitates or copies someone else's actions or ideas. The origin of this phrase is unclear, but it may be related to the idea of a cat copying the behavior of another animal.

- "Curiosity killed the cat" - used to warn people about the dangers of being too curious or inquisitive. This expression is used to warn people about the dangers of being too curious or inquisitive, and is often used when someone is asking too many questions. It is thought to have originated in the 16th century and was used to warn people about the dangers of being too curious about things that were best left unknown.

THINGS NAMED AFTER CATS

- ❖ Jaguar: A luxury car brand that was originally founded in England in 1922 as the Swallow Sidecar Company, and later became Jaguar Cars Limited in 1945. The brand is named after the jaguar, a big cat species known for its speed, strength, and grace.

- ❖ Cougar: A popular model of car produced by the Ford Motor Company from 1967 to 2002. The car was named after the cougar, also known as the puma or mountain lion, which is known for its agility and power.

- ❖ Puma: A brand of athletic shoes that was founded in Germany in 1948 and is known for its sleek design and innovative technology. The brand is named after the puma, which is also known as the cougar or mountain lion, and is known for its speed and agility.

- ❖ Leica: A brand of cameras that was founded in Germany in 1914 and is known for its high-quality lenses and precision engineering. The name "Leica" is derived from the founder's surname, Ernst Leitz, but it is also similar to the Latin word for "lynx," an animal commonly associated with vision and observation.

- ❖ Lynx: A brand of men's grooming products that was launched in the UK in 1995 and is known for its distinctive fragrance and stylish packaging. The brand is named after the lynx, a wildcat species that is known for its agility and stealth.

- ❖ Tiger Lily: A type of lily flower that is native to Asia and is known for its striking orange and black petals, which resemble the colors of a tiger.

The flower is often used in floral arrangements and is a popular choice for gardeners.

- ❖ The Cat-tail plant is a wetland herbaceous plant with tall, brownish spikes resembling a cat's tail. It is commonly used in floral arrangements, landscaping, and wetland restoration projects.
- ❖ Calico is a type of domestic cat with a distinctive coat pattern of orange, black, and white. This coat pattern has also been used to describe patterns in textiles and ceramics, where it is characterized by a mottled or spotted appearance.
- ❖ Black Cat Fireworks is a brand of fireworks named after the black cat, which is often associated with bad luck and superstition in many cultures. The brand was founded in China in the early 1900s and is now one of the largest producers of consumer fireworks in the United States.
- ❖ Panther chameleon: The Panther chameleon (Furcifer pardalis) is a species of chameleon native to Madagascar. They can grow up to 20 inches long and change color rapidly, as a form of communication and temperature regulation.
- ❖ Tiger balm: Tiger balm is a blend of natural ingredients like camphor, menthol, and clove oil that are traditionally used for pain relief. It was first developed in the 1870s in China and has since become popular around the world as a natural remedy for sore muscles, arthritis, and other ailments.
- ❖ The Lion's mane mushroom (Hericium erinaceus) is a type of edible mushroom that grows on the trunks of hardwood trees in North America, Europe, and Asia. The mushroom has a shaggy, mane-like appearance, which resembles the mane of a lion, hence the name.

CATS LOVE US EVEN THOUGH THEY DON'T LIKE TO SHOW IT

- ❖ Cats communicate their trust and affection through slow blinking. When a cat looks at you and slowly blinks, it's often referred to as a "kitty kiss." To strengthen your bond with your cat, try returning the gesture by slowly blinking back.

- Cats often groom each other as a sign of affection, and this behavior can extend to their human companions. If your cat licks you or gently nibbles on your skin, it's a sign they consider you part of their family.
- Cats have a higher body temperature than humans, and they love finding warm places to snuggle. If your cat chooses to sleep on your lap or next to you in bed, it's a sign of trust and affection.
- Cats knead their paws on soft surfaces, like your lap or a blanket, as a comforting behavior that harks back to their kittenhood. When your cat kneads and purrs on you, it's a sign that it trusts you.
- A cat named Baby saved her owner and the family dog from a house fire by biting her owner's arm and alerting her to the danger, showcasing the strong bond and protective instincts cats can have.
- A cat named Pudding alerted her new owner to a diabetic seizure just hours after being adopted. Pudding's quick actions saved her owner's life, solidifying their bond from day one.
- A woman's life was saved when her cat, Fidge, persistently pawed at her breast, prompting her to see a doctor. The early detection of cancer allowed for successful treatment, showcasing the extraordinary bond and intuition cats can have with their owners.
- A family's cat, Dexter, was lost during a devastating tornado in Oklahoma. Amazingly, he returned home 18 months later, demonstrating the unwavering loyalty cats can have for their families.
- A loyal cat named Toldo attended his owner's funeral, mourning his loss by bringing gifts to the gravesite. This heartwarming display highlighted the deep bond that can exist between cats and their owners.
- After going missing during a family vacation, Slinky Malinki traveled over 200 miles to return to his home. The determined cat's incredible journey captured the hearts of many and emphasized the depth of the human-cat bond.
- A cat named Tara bravely fought off a dog that was attacking a young boy, showcasing her protective instincts and the strong bond she shared with her family.

CATS ARE GOOD FOR YOU

- Interacting with cats can help lower stress levels and reduce anxiety by triggering the release of feel-good hormones like oxytocin.
- Studies have shown that cat owners have a lower risk of heart attack and stroke, as the calming effects of petting a cat can help lower blood pressure.
- Children exposed to cats in their early years are less likely to develop allergies and asthma, as their immune systems become more robust.
- Many cat owners report that they sleep better with their cat snuggled up beside them, as the cat's purring and presence can be soothing and comforting.
- Cats are natural predators and can help keep your home free of pests like mice and insects, serving as an eco-friendly and efficient form of pest control.
- Cats are generally low-maintenance compared to other pets, as they are independent and can groom themselves, making them a suitable companion for busy individuals.

CATS THAT SAVED LIVES

- In 2013, a cat named Tommy saved his owner's life when he woke her up during a gas leak in her home. The owner, who had lost her sense of smell due to cancer treatment, would not have known about the leak without Tommy's help.

- In 2019, a cat named Tilly saved her owner's life when she chased off a dog that was attacking the owner's small dog. Tilly was honored with the "Cat Hero" award from the Society for the Prevention of Cruelty to Animals.

- In 2010, a cat named Winnie saved her owner's life when she detected a blood clot in the owner's leg. Winnie kept pawing and meowing at the owner's leg until she went to the hospital, where doctors confirmed the blood clot and treated it in time.

- In 2015, a cat named Rascal saved a neighbor's life when he alerted his owner to a fire in the neighbor's home. Rascal's owner called 911, and the neighbor was able to escape the burning house thanks to Rascal's timely warning.

- In 2018, a cat named Smudge saved her owner's life when she detected a gas leak in their home. Smudge kept meowing and pawing at the owner until she realized something was wrong, and they were able to evacuate the house before any harm was done.

- In 2011, a cat named Muffy saved a family of four from a house fire in Connecticut. Muffy kept meowing and pawing at the door until the family woke up and realized what was happening, and they were able to escape the burning house unharmed.

- In 2017, a cat named Panda saved her owner's life when she alerted him to a carbon monoxide leak in their home. Panda kept meowing and pawing at the owner until he realized something was wrong, and they were able to get out of the house and call for help.

- In 2016, a cat named Joey saved his owner's life when he detected that she was having a stroke. Joey kept pawing and meowing at the owner until she was able to get help, and she made a full recovery thanks to his quick action.

- In 2012, a cat named Jessie saved a family of five from a house fire in England. Jessie kept meowing and pawing at the door until the family woke up and realized what was happening, and they were able to escape the burning house safely.

- In 2014, a cat named Boo Boo saved his owner's life when she had a seizure while walking near a canal in England. Boo Boo jumped onto the owner's chest and kept her head above water until rescuers arrived, saving her from drowning.

UNUSUAL BREEDS

- ❖ The Lykoi, or "werewolf cat," not only has a werewolf-like appearance but also exhibits some dog-like behaviors. They have a strong hunting instinct and can be seen wagging their tails when happy, making them a fascinating mix of feline and canine traits.
- ❖ The Devon Rex is known for its wavy, curly coat, which has been compared to that of an alien creature. These cats have large ears and a slender, almost alien-like appearance, earning them the nickname "E.T. cats."
- ❖ The hairless Sphynx cat is famous for its wrinkled, naked appearance. But did you know that despite being hairless, these cats can still get dandruff? Sphynx cats produce oil that would typically be absorbed by fur, but without fur, the oil can accumulate and cause skin flakes.
- ❖ The Manx breed is famous for its lack of tail, but this genetic mutation can sometimes result in "Manx Syndrome," a condition that causes spinal, bowel, and bladder problems. It's quite unusual for a breed to be both celebrated and burdened by its unique trait.
- ❖ Scottish Folds are known for their adorable folded ears, giving them an owl-like appearance. However, this ear folding is due to a genetic

mutation that can cause joint and cartilage disorders. Responsible breeding is crucial to minimize these health problems.

- ❖ The Toybob is a small breed of cat with a naturally short, kinked tail. Interestingly, this breed is the result of a spontaneous genetic mutation that occurred in Russia. Due to their tiny size, they are sometimes humorously referred to as "micro cats."

- ❖ The Cornish Rex has a soft, curly coat that resembles the texture of an old-fashioned carpet or a washboard. They are sometimes called the "Greyhound of cats" due to their slender body and arched back.

- ❖ The Burmilla breed was created by accident in the United Kingdom when a Chinchilla Persian and a Burmese cat were unintentionally allowed to mate. The resulting kittens were so attractive that a new breed was developed.

- ❖ The Sphynx-Scottish Fold mix is an unusual breed that merges the hairlessness of a Sphynx with the folded ears of a Scottish Fold. The result is a cat with a futuristic appearance, straight out of a science fiction movie.

- ❖ Nicknamed the "cat in sheep's clothing," the Selkirk Rex has a thick, curly coat that gives it a teddy bear-like appearance. Interestingly, their curly whiskers can sometimes make it challenging for them to sense their surroundings as effectively as other breeds.

- ❖ The Peterbald, a breed originating from St. Petersburg, Russia, is known for its hairless appearance and affectionate personality. They have a smooth, velvety skin that requires special care to maintain its softness.

- ❖ The LaPerm, a breed originating from the United States, is known for its curly and wavy fur that gives it a distinctive appearance. They are affectionate and playful, and are known for their sociability and adaptability.

- ❖ The Chausie, a breed created by breeding a domestic cat with a jungle cat, is known for its wild appearance and highly active personality. They are highly intelligent and social, and are prized for their trainability and adaptability.

- ❖ The Lykoi, a breed originating from Tennessee, USA, is known for its wolf-like appearance and energetic personality. They are highly active and playful, and are prized for their trainability and adaptability.

WILD FACTS ABOUT WILD CATS

- ❖ The fishing cat, found in South and Southeast Asia, is an excellent swimmer and has partially webbed feet, which helps it catch fish and other aquatic prey. They are one of the few cat species that enjoy water.
- ❖ The caracal, also known as the desert lynx, is known for its incredible leaping ability. They can jump up to 10 feet (3 meters) in the air to catch birds in flight, using their tufted ears to help them accurately locate prey.
- ❖ Black panthers are not a separate species; they are actually melanistic leopards or jaguars. The dark coloration is caused by an overproduction of melanin, giving their fur a black appearance with ghostly spots that can be seen in certain lighting conditions.
- ❖ Cheetahs are the fastest land animals, capable of reaching speeds up to 75 miles per hour (120 km/h) in short bursts. They also have non-retractable claws and specialized pads on their feet that help with traction while running.
- ❖ The smallest wild cat species is the rusty-spotted cat found in India and Sri Lanka. They weigh only 2 to 3.5 pounds (0.9 to 1.6 kg) and are about the size of a domestic cat.
- ❖ The sand cat, native to the deserts of Africa and Asia, has fur-covered foot pads that protect their paws from the hot sand. They are also expert diggers, creating burrows to escape the desert heat.

- The margay, a small wild cat found in Central and South America, has the unique ability to rotate its hind legs 180 degrees. This allows them to climb down trees headfirst and hang from branches by one hind leg.
- The clouded leopard has the largest canine teeth relative to body size among all cats. They are sometimes referred to as "modern-day saber-toothed cats" due to their impressive fangs, which can be as long as 1.8 inches (4.5 cm).
- The serval, native to Africa, has the longest legs relative to body size of any cat species. Their large ears and long legs give them excellent hearing and jumping abilities, allowing them to detect and catch prey with ease.
- The Pallas's cat, found in Central Asia, has round pupils, unlike most other wild cats with slit-like pupils. Their flat face and dense fur give them a distinctive appearance, making them look like a grumpy, fluffy ball.

HYBRID BREEDS: HALF-CAT, HALF CHOCOLATE?

- York Chocolate is a spontaneous creation, originating from a cross between a black domestic shorthair and a Siamese. York Chocolates have a rich, chocolate-brown coat and striking green eyes, making them look like a luxurious, feline version of a chocolate bar.
- A cross between a domestic cat and a serval, Savannah cats have been known to mimic the behavior of dogs, including playing fetch and going

for walks on a leash. They can even jump up to 8 feet high from a standing position!

- Bengals are a hybrid between the Asian leopard cat and a domestic cat. Some Bengal cats have an unusual trait called "glittering," where their fur appears to sparkle in the sunlight due to the hollow structure of their hair shafts.

- Chausies are a hybrid breed, a mix between a domestic cat and a jungle cat. Chausies are known for their love of water and have been known to join their owners in the shower, much to the surprise of bathers.

- A mix between a Bengal and an Ocicat, the Cheetoh was created to resemble a wild cheetah, complete with spots and a lean body. Despite their wild appearance, Cheetoh cats are known for their friendly and affectionate nature.

- The Serengeti is a hybrid breed created by crossing a Bengal with an Oriental Shorthair. The breed was developed to resemble the African serval, but without using any actual serval genes. Serengetis are known for their extreme athleticism and high energy levels.

- A rare and controversial hybrid, the Caracat is a cross between a domestic cat and a caracal. These cats have the long legs and tufted ears of the caracal, as well as a bold and assertive personality. Due to ethical concerns and regulations, Caracats are not widely available or recognized as a breed.

- The Highlander breed is a mix between a domestic cat and a Jungle Curl. These cats have distinct curled ears, a short tail, and a muscular body. Their playful nature and unusual appearance often draw comparisons to the mythical creatures of fantasy novels.

- Pixie-bobs are a breed created by crossing a domestic cat with a North American bobcat. They have a short tail and a wild appearance, but their personality is typically gentle and friendly.

- An extremely rare and controversial hybrid, the Jaglion is a cross between a male jaguar and a female lion. While not a domestic cat breed, the existence of the Jaglion highlights the surprising genetic compatibility of some big cat species. These hybrids are not found in the wild and have only been bred in captivity under unique circumstances.

- A green cat was born in Denmark in 1995. Some people believe that high levels of copper in the water pipes nearby may have given his fur a verdigris effect.

FELINE GENIUSES

- ❖ Cats have individual preferences for different music genres, suggesting they have the cognitive ability to process and appreciate various auditory stimuli.

- ❖ A study published in the journal Animal Cognition found that cats can predict the presence of an object hidden in a container based on the noise it makes when shaken. This demonstrates that cats have an understanding of cause and effect, as well as object permanence.

- ❖ A study at the University of Oxford found that cats can learn to manipulate simple mechanisms, such as levers and latches, by observing other cats or humans. This demonstrates that cats possess social learning abilities, which were previously thought to be unique to primates and certain bird species.

- ❖ Cats have excellent long-term memory, and they can remember the location of hidden objects for up to 16 hours. This ability is helpful for hunting and navigation in their natural environment.

- ❖ Cats are known to have an internal clock that allows them to anticipate regular events, such as meal times or their owner's arrival home. This sense of time helps them adapt to routines and maintain a sense of security.

- ❖ A study published in the journal Applied Animal Behaviour Science found that cats can solve problems by applying previously learned rules to new situations. In the study, cats were trained to pull a string to access food, and then later presented with a new, more complex string-pulling task, which they were able to solve.

- ❖ The Morris water maze is a well-known test of spatial memory and learning, typically used with rats and mice, and it has been adapted for use with cats. Cats have been shown to perform well in this test, demonstrating their ability to learn and remember the location of a hidden platform in a pool of water.

- ❖ Although cats do not typically recognize themselves in mirrors, they can use mirrors to locate hidden objects, suggesting that they understand the concept of reflection. This ability has been demonstrated in various studies and highlights the adaptability of feline cognition.

- ❖ A cat named Koko, owned by a deaf woman, reportedly learned to communicate using American Sign Language. Koko would use her paws to mimic the signs her owner used, such as making the sign for "food" when she was hungry. While this story may be anecdotal, it illustrates the remarkable ability of cats to adapt and learn from their environment.

- ❖ Cats have been known to open doors, windows, and unlock cages to escape or access food, displaying their intelligence and determination.

CATS KNOW THINGS BEFORE YOU DO

- ❖ Cats have a keen sense of vibration and can often detect earthquakes before they happen, making them natural furry seismologists.

- ❖ Cats are known to be sensitive to human moods and emotions, sometimes offering comfort or companionship when their owners are feeling down, showcasing their empathic abilities.

- ❖ A cat's memory is so precise that they can remember exact locations for extended periods, even if they've only visited the spot once. This makes them excellent at retracing their steps or finding hidden treasures.

- ❖ Cats can differentiate between various shades of color, contrary to the popular belief that they only see in black and white. However, their color vision is limited compared to humans, so they see the world in a slightly different, more pastel palette.

- ❖ Some cats have an uncanny ability to predict weather changes, often seeking shelter or becoming more restless just before a storm or temperature shift, making them natural feline meteorologists.

- Cats have a unique ability to land on their feet, known as the "righting reflex." This skill is so well-developed that even kittens as young as three weeks old can begin to exhibit this acrobatic talent.
- Cats are skilled climbers and can scale vertical surfaces, such as trees or walls, with ease. This is due to their retractable claws, strong hind legs, and innate sense of balance, making them the ultimate feline mountaineers.

MEMORY AND EMOTION

- Cats can "catch" emotions from their owners, becoming stressed or calm depending on their owner's emotional state, demonstrating their ability to empathize with humans.
- Cats can grieve the loss of a fellow feline companion or their owner, sometimes displaying behavioral changes such as decreased appetite or increased vocalization, showing they form deep emotional bonds.
- Cats can remember the locations of their favorite hiding spots, food sources, and even the litter box, demonstrating their impressive spatial memory.
- Cats can remember and recall past experiences, such as traumatic events, and may display signs of fear or anxiety when faced with similar situations, highlighting their long-term memory capabilities.
- Cats are capable of detecting and responding to subtle changes in their owner's facial expressions, showing that they can pick up on human emotions and adjust their behavior accordingly.
- Cats can display signs of jealousy when a new pet or family member is introduced, seeking extra attention or acting out to regain their social status, proving they are sensitive to changes in their social environment.
- Cats purr not only when they are content but also when they are stressed or in pain, suggesting that purring serves as a form of emotional self-regulation to calm themselves down.
- Cats often seek out physical contact with their owners or other cats when they feel anxious or scared, showing that they rely on social bonds to help regulate their emotions and provide a sense of security.

DO YOU CHOOSE A CAT, OR DOES A CAT CHOOSE YOU?

- ❖ The Sphynx cat, known for its hairlessness, often needs to wear clothes to stay warm. If you love dressing up your pets, a Sphynx might be your perfect fashion-forward companion.
- ❖ Cats were once believed to influence political decisions. In ancient Egypt, people observed which paw a cat used to reach for food, and if the cat used its right paw, it was considered a good omen for important decisions.
- ❖ If you're looking for a cat to snuggle with, consider the affectionate and cuddly Ragdoll, known for its tendency to go limp in your arms like a ragdoll when picked up.
- ❖ The position of a cat's bed can impact their personality. Cats that sleep near windows tend to be more curious and outgoing, while those that prefer hidden spots may be more introverted.
- ❖ Some cat breeds, like the Abyssinian and Bengal, are known for their high energy levels and need for mental stimulation, making them perfect companions for active households or those looking for a feline workout buddy.
- ❖ Siamese cats are known for their "chatty" nature, often engaging in conversations with their owners through a series of vocalizations. If you want a talkative companion, a Siamese might be the perfect choice.

- Some cats, like the Maine Coon and Norwegian Forest Cat, have a strong instinct for climbing. If you have tall furniture or trees, be prepared for your feline friend to explore every nook and cranny.

CAT HOUSES (NO, NOT THAT KIND!)

- In ancient Egypt, people provided their cats with intricately designed homes made of wood, clay, or stone, often adorned with hieroglyphs, showcasing their admiration for these revered creatures.
- The world's oldest surviving cat house, which dates back to the 15th century, can be found in the historic town of Kilkenny, Ireland. This ancient structure has housed countless feline inhabitants throughout the centuries.
- Some famous architects have designed cat houses. Frank Lloyd Wright, for example, designed a custom home for a client's cat, complete with geometric shapes and a ramp, reflecting his signature style.
- Cat-loving celebrities often provide luxurious homes for their feline friends. Taylor Swift's cats have their own room, complete with a pink canopy bed and custom cat furniture.
- Luxury cat hotels, or "cat resorts," offer lavish accommodations for feline guests, including individual suites, spa treatments, and gourmet dining options, providing a home away from home for pampered pets.
- The Cat House on the Kings in California is the largest no-cage, no-kill cat sanctuary and adoption center, providing a comfortable and spacious home for over 700 cats.
- Cat cafes, where customers can enjoy a beverage while interacting with resident cats, often provide homes for cats in need. Some, like Lady Dinah's Cat Emporium in London, have become famous tourist attractions.
- Events like the annual Architects for Animals "Giving Shelter" fundraiser challenge architects and designers to create innovative and functional cat homes, raising awareness about homeless cats and supporting animal welfare organizations.
- The world's tallest cat tree, measuring over 21 feet in height, provides an impressive home for adventurous felines, allowing them to climb, perch, and explore to their heart's content.

DID MY CAT JUST MANIPULATE ME?

- ❖ Some cats love to "scratch" records, making their owners wonder if they have a feline DJ in the making. This behavior is actually a way for cats to mark their territory and maintain their claws.

- ❖ Some cats prefer to drink from a running faucet, making their owners act as personal water butlers by turning on the tap when they're thirsty.

- ❖ Cats can inherit a gene that makes them sensitive to catnip, causing them to exhibit playful or even euphoric behavior when exposed to this herb. However, not all cats are affected, making some feline friends immune to the allure of catnip.

- ❖ Believe it or not, some cats can be toilet trained, and there are even specialized training kits available to help teach your feline friend how to use the porcelain throne.

- ❖ Cats are known to be finicky eaters, often insisting on eating from a specific bowl or preferring one brand of cat food over another. Some cats will even stage a hunger strike until their preferred meal is served.

- ❖ Cats can become captivated by nature documentaries or videos featuring birds and small animals. Some owners even curate a feline-friendly TV playlist to keep their cat entertained.

- ❖ Cats can experience "whisker stress" if their food or water bowls are too narrow, causing their whiskers to touch the sides. This may lead to picky eating or other behavioral issues, so be sure to provide wide, shallow dishes for your cat's meals.

- Some cat owners have trained their cats to walk on a leash or even use a treadmill to help them stay active and maintain a healthy weight.

UNDERSTANDING FELINE BODY LANGUAGE

- When a cat raises its rear end while being petted, it's actually a sign of trust and appreciation, not an invitation to scratch their behind.
- When a cat arches its back and puffs up its fur, it's trying to make itself look larger and more intimidating in response to a perceived threat.
- If a cat rolls over and shows you their belly, it's a sign of trust and vulnerability. However, it doesn't always mean they want a belly rub – proceed with caution!
- Cats sometimes chatter their teeth when they see prey outside (like birds). This behavior is thought to be a form of frustration or excitement, as they can't reach their target.
- When a cat rubs its head against you, it's marking you with pheromones from glands on their face, essentially claiming you as their own.
- When cats don't cover their poop, it is seen as a sign of aggression, meaning they don't fear you.
- A cat might twirl around your legs when they're excited or happy to see you. This is their way of saying "hello" and showing affection.
- When a cat opens its mouth and curls back its upper lip, it is actually using the Jacobson's organ to analyze scents in its environment.
- When a cat tucks its paws and tail underneath its body, resembling a loaf of bread, it usually means they feel comfortable and secure in their environment.
- A slow blink is a "kitty kiss." This movement shows contentment and trust.
- If your cat approaches you with a straight, almost vibrating tail, this means that she is extremely happy to see you.
- Cats have a unique "vocabulary" with their owner — each cat has a different set of vocalizations, purrs and behaviors.
- Cats find it threatening when you make direct eye contact with them.
- Cats mark you as their territory when they rub their faces and bodies against you, as they have scent glands in those areas.

- Hissing is defensive, not aggressive. It's an expression of fear, stress or discomfort of a threatened cat communicating "stay away."
- If cats are fighting, the cat that's hissing is the more vulnerable one.
- Kneading — which some people refer to as "making biscuits" — is a sign of contentment and happiness. Cats knead their mothers when they are nursing to stimulate the let-down of milk.
- Meowing is a behavior that cats developed exclusively to communicate with people.
- When cats hit you with retracted claws, they're playing, not attacking.
- When dogs wag their tails, they may be expressing happiness. But this isn't the case for cats! When your cat wags her tail, it's her way of warning you that you are getting on her nerves.
- When your cat sticks his butt in your face, he is doing so as a gesture of friendship.
- Whiskers are also good indicators of a cat's mood. When a cat is scared, he put his whiskers back. But when a cat is in hunting mode, he puts his whiskers forward.
- Cats often attack your ankles when they're bored.
- Male cats who try to get to a female in heat can show very bizarre behavior — for example, some have been known to slide down chimneys!

TAIL SIGNALS

- A quivering or vibrating tail can indicate excitement or anticipation, such as when a cat is about to pounce on a toy or catch prey.
- A slow swishing tail can indicate that a cat is relaxed and content, enjoying the company of their owner or other cats.
- A quick, sharp twitch of the tail can indicate irritation or annoyance, such as when a cat is being bothered by something or someone.
- A puffed-up, bushy tail can indicate fear or aggression, and is often seen when a cat feels threatened or intimidated.
- A slow, sweeping tail movement can indicate that a cat is curious or interested in something, such as a new toy or scent.

- ❖ Your cat drapes its tail over another cat, your dog, or you as a symbol of friendship.
- ❖ A rapidly flicking tail can indicate that a cat is feeling agitated or anxious, and may be a sign that they need some alone time to calm down.
- ❖ A tail held high and curved at the tip can indicate that a cat is feeling happy and confident, and is often seen when they are greeting their owner or other cats.
- ❖ A tail held low and tucked between the legs can indicate fear or submission, and is often seen when a cat is feeling threatened or intimidated.
- ❖ A tail that is twitching or quivering at the base can indicate that a cat is feeling particularly excited or aroused, such as when they are about to mate or hunt.
- ❖ A tail that is held stiffly and straight up can indicate that a cat is feeling alert and ready to react to any potential danger or threat.

TRANSLATING CAT SOUNDS

- ❖ Just like humans, cats can develop regional "accents" or dialects. Depending on the area they live in and the people they interact with, cats can develop unique vocalizations that are specific to their environment.

- Cats often meow as a means of communication with humans, not with other cats. Adult cats rarely meow at each other, as they rely on body language, facial expressions, and scent for communication.
- The "silent meow" is a unique and adorable phenomenon where a cat appears to meow without making any sound. This is often used to get their human's attention or to make a request without being too demanding.
- Cats can modulate their vocalizations to mimic the pitch and intensity of a human baby's cry, which increases the likelihood of their owners responding to their needs. This is known as "solicitation purring."
- Each cat's meow is unique, and they can develop personalized meows to communicate with their specific human companions. As a result, owners often become experts at interpreting their cat's individual sounds.
- Cats are highly adaptable and can learn to associate specific sounds or vocalizations with particular actions or events. For example, a cat may learn that a specific meow will get them food, while another meow will get them a head scratch.
- Cats' vocalizations can be influenced by their breed, personality, and individual experiences. For instance, Siamese cats are known for being more vocal than other breeds, often engaging in loud and lengthy "conversations" with their owners.
- Cats can understand the tone of your voice better than the words you're saying. They are sensitive to the pitch and intensity of human speech and can distinguish between friendly and threatening vocalizations.
- Cats may use different vocalizations to communicate with different members of the family. They might have a specific meow for their primary caregiver, another for a secondary caregiver, and even a separate one for younger family members.
- Cats can adjust their vocalizations over time to better communicate with their human companions. They may develop new sounds or modify existing ones to more effectively convey their needs and desires.
- Cats use a range of different purring frequencies for different purposes. The healing purr, which is around 25-50 Hz, has been shown to help reduce inflammation and promote tissue regeneration in both cats and humans.

- Cats can mimic other animals' sounds. Some cat owners have reported their cats imitating birds, rodents, or even other cats to try and manipulate their environment or prey.
- Mother cats use short, high-pitched sounds, a cross between a meow and a purr, to communicate with their kittens and sometimes with their humans as well. These sounds are used for mother-kitten communication.
- The purring of a cheetah is quite distinct from that of a domestic cat. Cheetahs have a unique purring sound that is more like a series of rapid, high-pitched chirps, which is thought to serve as a form of communication between mother cheetahs and their cubs.

CATS CAN TALK WITH OTHER SPECIES

- In Australia, a cat named Jasper befriended a group of wild kangaroos and was often seen playing and hopping around with them.
- A domestic cat in California named Baloo formed a close bond with a group of dogs at an animal shelter, often napping and grooming with them.
- Bella, a cat living in England, became friends with a group of cows on a local farm, and would often sleep in the hay bales alongside them.
- A cat named Boots in Florida was spotted swimming and playing with wild dolphins in a nearby lagoon.
- In New Zealand, a cat named Gandalf made friends with a group of goats on a local farm, and would often play with them and try to eat their food.
- Sable, a cat in Canada, formed an unlikely friendship with a group of wild deer, and would often sit with them and share their food.
- A cat named Toby in Australia was often seen following a group of wild emus and even trying to imitate their calls.
- Milo, a cat in New York, became friends with a group of squirrels in a park, often sitting with them and watching them gather nuts.
- In South Africa, a cat named Simba played with a group of wild meerkats and even tried to help them catch insects.

- In Germany, a cat named Felix was seen sitting and sharing food with a group of wild hedgehogs in the garden.

PLAY TIME

- Cats have a unique "play face" during high-energy play sessions. Their pupils dilate, and their ears may twitch or flatten slightly.
- Cats use play as a way to establish social hierarchies. Dominant cats typically initiate play more often and control the pace and intensity of the play session.
- Cats have different play styles based on their personalities. Some cats prefer to play alone, while others enjoy interactive play with their humans or other cats.
- Cats have been known to form friendships with other species, including dogs, rabbits, and even birds. These interspecies relationships often involve play and grooming behaviors.
- Cats can become overstimulated during play, leading to aggression or biting. To avoid this, it's important to monitor their body language and use toys that allow for distance between your hands and the cat, such as wand toys or laser pointers.
- The "crazy time" or "zoomies" that many cat owners witness is a burst of energy that cats experience, often resulting in high-speed laps around the house. This behavior is believed to help cats burn off excess energy and practice their hunting skills.

- Cats have an innate "play" program that includes a sequence of behaviors: stalking, chasing, pouncing, biting, and finally "killing." These behaviors help them hone their hunting skills, even if they're only hunting toys.

- Despite being solitary hunters, cats can form complex social groups called "clowders" in the wild. These groups often consist of related females and their offspring, and they engage in cooperative care and grooming.

- Kitten "kindergarten" is a real thing. Some animal behaviorists and veterinarians recommend socialization classes for young kittens to help them develop proper social skills and reduce future behavior problems.

- Cats can become "friends" with their reflection in a mirror, treating their reflection as a playmate or social companion. This behavior demonstrates their ability to adapt to unusual social situations.

- Some cats are known to "dunk" their toys in their water bowls, a behavior that may be related to their instinct to move prey to a safe location before consuming it.

- In a study published in the journal Applied Animal Behaviour Science, researchers found that cats preferred toys that were interactive and allowed them to play with their owners, rather than toys that they could play with alone.

- A recent news story reported that a cat named Simba was caught on camera playing a game of fetch with his owner. The video went viral on social media, with many viewers expressing surprise and delight at the sight of a cat playing fetch like a dog.

- Another study published in the journal Animal Cognition found that cats have the ability to understand cause and effect relationships, and can even predict the movement of objects in order to catch them during play.

- According to a study published in the journal PLoS ONE, cats who play with their owners are more likely to form secure attachment bonds, which can improve their overall well-being.

- In a recent news story, a cat named Suki was filmed playing a game of hide-and-seek with her owner. The video quickly went viral, with many viewers expressing surprise and delight at the sight of a cat playing such a complex game.

FELINE OLYMPICS

- Ziggy the cat, a Bengal from the United States, gained popularity for his exceptional agility skills. His owner, Molly DeVoss, shared videos of Ziggy navigating a homemade obstacle course in their living room. Ziggy's impressive feats included climbing up a ladder, jumping through hoops, and even walking a tightrope.

- The Cat Fanciers' Association (CFA) organized a cat agility competition in 2011 where a cat named Gizmo stunned the audience with his speed and precision. Gizmo, a brown tabby domestic shorthair, completed the entire course in just 12 seconds, setting a record that left the audience in awe.

- In Japan, a cat named Nya-Suke became an internet sensation for his incredible jumping ability. His owner posted videos of Nya-Suke leaping incredible heights to reach various objects, including soaring over a 6.5-foot barrier. Nya-Suke's remarkable athleticism and agility garnered widespread attention and demonstrated the true potential of feline agility.

- In 2017, an event called "CatCon" was held in Los Angeles, featuring a cat agility course as one of its main attractions. One of the most memorable moments of the event was when a cat named Smokey, dressed as a pirate, successfully navigated the course while wearing his costume, delighting the audience with his agility and determination.

- A cat named Twyla from Oregon, who was born without her front legs, became an inspiration to many when she learned to navigate an agility course using only her hind legs and tail for balance. Twyla's remarkable story, resilience, and agility skills have been featured in various media outlets, showing that even cats with disabilities can excel in agility with the right training and support.

- While cat agility competitions are less common than dog agility events, they are gaining popularity worldwide, with events being held in countries like the United States, Canada, Japan, and the United Kingdom.

- Cat agility courses sometimes include water-based obstacles, like shallow pools or fountains, which can be both challenging and entertaining for cats and spectators alike.

- Many cat breeds can excel in agility, but some breeds, like Abyssinians, Bengals, and Siamese, are particularly well-suited for these activities due to their high energy levels and athletic abilities.

CATS THAT ARE FAMOUS FOR HOLDING WORLD RECORDS

- ❖ World's most expensive cat collar: The world's most expensive cat collar is made by a jewelry company called Amour Amour and is encrusted with over 1,000 diamonds, with a price tag of $3.2 million.
- ❖ World's longest cat: The current record holder for the world's longest cat is Barivel, a Maine Coon who measures 120 cm (3 feet, 11.2 inches) from nose to tail.
- ❖ World's heaviest cat: The heaviest cat on record was Himmy, an Australian cat who weighed 21.3 kg (46.8 lbs) at his heaviest.
- ❖ World's loudest purr: The cat with the world's loudest purr is a tabby named Smokey, who has a purr that measures up to 67.7 decibels.
- ❖ World's most toes on a cat: A polydactyl cat named Jake holds the record for the most toes on a cat, with a total of 28 toes (7 on each paw).
- ❖ World's tallest cat: The current record holder for the world's tallest cat is Arcturus Aldebaran Powers, a Savannah cat who measures 48.4 cm (19.05 inches) tall.
- ❖ World's fastest cat: The world's fastest cat is the cheetah, which can reach speeds of up to 70 miles per hour.
- ❖ World's most expensive cat: A Bengal cat named Zeus holds the record for the most expensive cat ever sold, with a price tag of $154,000.

- World's largest cat painting: A painting of a cat by Chinese artist Xiaoyun He holds the record for the world's largest cat painting, measuring 15.86 meters (52 feet) long and 5.6 meters (18 feet) tall.
- World's largest cat litter: The world's largest cat litter was made by Fresh Step in 2014 and weighed 4,409 kg (9,728 lbs).
- World's most traveled cat: A cat named Hamlet holds the record for the most traveled cat, having visited 51 countries over the course of his life.
- World's longest whiskers on a cat: A Maine Coon cat named Missi had the world's longest whiskers on a cat, measuring 19 cm (7.5 inches) long.
- World's most prolific mother cat: A cat named Dusty holds the record for the most kittens born to a single cat, with a total of 420 kittens over her lifetime.
- World's fastest cat on two legs: A cat named Alley holds the record for the fastest cat on two legs, running a distance of 100 feet in just 6.56 seconds.
- World's most watched cat video: The video "Nyan Cat" holds the record for the most watched cat video on the internet, with over 180 million views.
- World's most expensive cat food: The world's most expensive cat food is the "Fillets of Feline" dish, which costs $100 per serving and is made with quail eggs, salmon, and lobster.
- World's largest cat statue: A statue of a cat in Japan holds the record for the world's largest cat statue, measuring 41.8 meters (137 feet) tall.
- The cat with the most recorded mouse kills is a Siamese named Tommaso, who killed more than 2,000 mice in his lifetime.
- The cat with the most recorded mouse kills is a Siamese named Tommaso, who killed more than 2,000 mice in his lifetime.
- The cat with the longest recorded nap is a Persian named Pooka, who slept for an incredible 18 hours and 15 minutes.
- The cat with the most recorded catches of a laser pointer in one minute is a Bengal cat named Flash, who caught an incredible 25 laser points. How this cat was able to catch laser light is a mystery!

CAT SHOWS AND COMPETITIONS

- ❖ The first cat show was held at the Crystal Palace in London in 1871, featuring over 170 cats of various breeds. It was organized by Harrison Weir, who is considered the "Father of the Cat Fancy."

- ❖ The "Supreme Cat Show," organized by the Governing Council of the Cat Fancy (GCCF) in the United Kingdom, is one of the largest cat shows in the world. It is often referred to as the "Crufts of the cat world," a reference to the famous dog show.

- ❖ In Russia, an annual cat costume contest called "Cats in Hats" takes place, where owners dress their feline friends in elaborate costumes and accessories, showcasing their creativity and love for their pets.

- ❖ The Hemingway Home and Museum in Key West, Florida, hosts an annual "Hemingway Look-Alike Contest" in honor of the author Ernest Hemingway. One of the unique aspects of this event is the presence of around 40-50 polydactyl (six-toed) cats that roam the property, as Hemingway himself was known to have a fondness for these unusual felines.

- ❖ In Japan, the "Nekobiyaka" cat café holds regular "Cat Elections," where visitors vote for their favorite feline resident. The winning cat earns the title of "Prime Minister" and receives special treats and privileges.

- ❖ The Algonquin Hotel in New York City has had a long-standing tradition of hosting an annual cat fashion show. The event, which began in the

1930s, features feline models dressed in elaborate costumes and raises money for animal welfare organizations.

❖ The "World Championship Cat Show," hosted by the World Cat Federation, is held annually in a different country each year. This prestigious event draws thousands of cats and their owners from around the world, competing for various titles and awards.

❖ An annual event in Belgium called the "Kattenstoet" (Cat Parade) celebrates all things feline, including a cat beauty contest. This unusual festival originated in the Middle Ages and features elaborate costumes, floats, and street performances dedicated to cats.

❖ In 2011, a cat named Hank from Virginia made headlines when he "ran" for the United States Senate. Hank's campaign, which was a creative way to raise awareness for animal welfare issues, even had its merchandise, website, and social media presence. While Hank didn't win the election, he did manage to garner over 6,000 votes.

OUTDOOR ADVENTURES WITH CATS

❖ In France, a daring cat unknowingly stowed away on a hang glider, clinging to the wing as it soared into the sky. The pilot and cat both landed safely, making for a humorous and unexpected adventure.

❖ In Russia, a stray cat named Masha discovered an abandoned baby in a cardboard box during a freezing winter night. Masha climbed into the box and kept the baby warm until help arrived, saving the infant's life.

- A rescue cat named Quandary Q Lotus Lady, also known as "QQ," became famous for her hiking adventures in Colorado. QQ has scaled over 40 mountain peaks, proving that even cats can be outdoor enthusiasts and mountaineers.
- In the UK, a cat named Theo saved his owner's life when she suffered a blood clot. Theo sensed something was wrong and persistently pawed at her until she awoke, enabling her to call for help. Theo was awarded the National Cat of the Year Award for his heroic actions.
- In 2013, a cat named Holly became separated from her owners during a vacation in Florida. Determined to return home, Holly traveled an astonishing 1,200 miles over two months, finally reuniting with her family in West Palm Beach.
- A cat named Nala took to the skies with her owner, an experienced paraglider, in a custom-made harness. Nala's adventures have been captured on video, showcasing the brave cat's aerial escapades.
- In 2006, a cat named Tommy accidentally dialed 911, potentially saving his owner's life during a medical emergency. While it's unclear how Tommy managed to dial the number, his actions led to emergency responders arriving on the scene in time to help.

TOYS FOR CATS (OR FOR HUMANS?)

- Wand toys: These toys consist of a long wand with a feather, toy mouse, or other object attached to the end. They allow you to simulate the movement of prey and engage your cat in interactive play.
- Laser pointers: Cats love chasing the red dot created by laser pointers, and this can be a great way to provide them with exercise and mental stimulation. However, it's important to never shine the laser directly into your cat's eyes.
- Catnip toys: Many cats are attracted to catnip, a herb that has a stimulating effect on some felines. Catnip toys can be a fun way to provide your cat with sensory stimulation and playtime.
- Puzzle toys: These toys are designed to challenge your cat's problem-solving skills and provide mental stimulation. Puzzle toys can come in various forms, such as treat dispensers or balls with hidden compartments.

- Balls: Simple balls can be a great toy for cats, especially if they have a bell or other noise-making mechanism inside. Cats enjoy chasing and batting around balls, which can provide them with exercise and entertainment.

- Cardboard boxes: While not a traditional toy, cardboard boxes can provide endless entertainment for cats. They can play, nap, and hide in boxes, which can be a fun and affordable way to provide them with playtime.

- Automated toys: There are various automated toys available for cats, such as self-moving balls or robotic mice. These toys can provide cats with entertainment and exercise even when you're not able to play with them.

- Feather toys: Feather toys can be a fun way to simulate prey and engage your cat in interactive play. Feather toys can come in various forms, such as wand toys or balls with feathers attached.

- Crinkle toys: Many cats are attracted to toys that make noise, and crinkle toys can be a fun way to provide sensory stimulation and playtime.

- Tunnels: Tunnels can be a fun way to provide cats with exercise and entertainment. Cats can run through tunnels, hide inside them, and play peek-a-boo with their owners.

WORLD'S WEIRDEST CAT PRODUCTS

- The cat wigs, or "cat toupees", were invented by a company called "Cat Atelier", and they were inspired by the trend of dressing up cats in cosplay costumes. They come in a variety of colors and styles, and they are made of soft synthetic hair that is safe for cats.

- The catnip bubbles were invented by a company called "Bubbletastic", and they are made of non-toxic ingredients that are safe for cats to ingest. The bubbles are scented with catnip oil, which can make your cat go wild with excitement.

- The cat-sized DJ scratching pad was invented by a company called "Suck UK", and it is designed to look like a real DJ turntable. The pad has a scratch pad on one side and a mixer on the other side, and it comes with a cardboard box that looks like a DJ booth.

- The cat treadmill was invented by a company called "One Fast Cat", and it is designed to give your cat a cardio workout without taking up too much space in your home. The treadmill is made of durable plastic and has a textured surface to help your cat grip it.

- ❖ The cat-shaped cake molds were invented by a company called "Wilton", and they are made of non-stick silicone that is easy to clean. The molds come in different shapes and sizes, including a sitting cat, a lying cat, and a cat face.
- ❖ The cat grass growing kits were invented by a company called "Smart Cat", and they are designed to provide your cat with a natural source of fiber and nutrients. The kits come with seeds, soil, and a growing container, and they can be used indoors or outdoors.
- ❖ The cat selfie stick was invented by a company called "PetSafe", and it is designed to help you take better photos of your cat. The stick has a little toy mouse on the end that can get your cat's attention, and it is adjustable to different angles.
- ❖ The cat treat dispenser was invented by a company called "PetSafe", and it is designed to be activated by your cat's paw.
- ❖ The cat face massager was invented by a company called "Petting Pal", and it is designed to help your cat relax and reduce stress. The massager has little silicone nubs that can massage your cat's face and neck, and it can be used on both cats and dogs.
- ❖ The cat toilet training kit was invented by a company called "CitiKitty", and it is designed to help you train your cat to use the toilet like a human. The kit comes with a special toilet seat that fits over your regular toilet seat, and it has different stages to help your cat get used to the idea of using the toilet.
- ❖ Cat wine: A non-alcoholic beverage made specifically for cats, often made from catnip, beets, and other natural ingredients.
- ❖ Cat grass planter: A small indoor planter designed for growing grass specifically for cats to nibble on and play with.
- ❖ Cat onesie: A snug-fitting, full-body garment designed to be worn by cats, often used for warmth or for play.
- ❖ Cat wheel: A large, rotating wheel designed for cats to run and play on, similar to a hamster wheel.

GAMES AND ACTIVITIES FOR CAT AND "OWNER"

- ❖ Build a cat fort. Use cardboard boxes, blankets, and other materials to build a fort or playhouse for your cat. Your cat can explore and play in the fort, and you can add toys and treats to make it even more enticing.
- ❖ Create an obstacle course. Set up an obstacle course for your cat using items around your home, such as boxes, pillows, and blankets. Encourage your cat to jump, climb, and explore the course with treats and toys.
- ❖ Go on a nature walk. Take your cat on a nature walk, using a cat harness or carrier. Your cat can experience the sights and smells of the outdoors while still being safely contained.
- ❖ Practice cat yoga. Try practicing yoga with your cat, using poses that incorporate your cat's natural movements, such as downward-facing cat or cat-cow pose.
- ❖ Play hide-and-seek. Play a game of hide-and-seek with your cat, hiding treats or toys around your home for your cat to find.
- ❖ Have a movie night. Settle in for a movie night with your cat, choosing films or TV shows that feature cats or other animals. Your cat can snuggle up with you on the couch while you watch.
- ❖ Make cat-friendly crafts. Create cat-friendly crafts, such as a catnip toy or a cardboard scratching post, using materials that are safe for your cat to play with.

- Have a photo shoot. Set up a photo shoot with your cat, using props and costumes to create fun and memorable images.
- Take a cat-friendly road trip. Take a road trip with your cat, using a cat carrier or harness to keep them safe and secure. Explore new places and enjoy the journey together.

CLASSIC CAT BOOKS AND STORIES

- "The Black Cat" is a short story by Edgar Allan Poe that is about a man who becomes obsessed with his cat and eventually murders it.
- The first book in English literature to feature a cat as a central character is "The Master Cat, or Puss in Boots," which was published in 1697.
- The world's oldest surviving illustrated book about cats is "Ippo-shū," which was written in Japan in the early 12th century.
- The famous children's book "The Cat in the Hat" by Dr. Seuss was written as a response to a challenge to create a book that could help children learn to read.
- In ancient Egypt, cats were revered as sacred animals and were often depicted in paintings and sculptures.
- The world's largest cat book collection belongs to a man named Harold Sims, who has over 30,000 books about cats in his collection.
- Ernest Hemingway was a famous cat lover and owned over 50 cats during his lifetime.

- ❖ The Cheshire Cat from Lewis Carroll's "Alice's Adventures in Wonderland" is known for its distinctive grin, which inspired the phrase "grinning like a Cheshire Cat."
- ❖ The world's smallest cat book is called "Old Possum's Book of Practical Cats" by T.S. Eliot and measures just 1.5 inches by 1 inch.
- ❖ The world's longest cat book is called "The History of Cats" by Brian Vesey-Fitzgerald and contains over 560 pages of information about cats.
- ❖ The famous cat detective, Koko, in the "Cat Who" series by Lillian Jackson Braun, was inspired by the author's own cat, KoKo.
- ❖ "A Street Cat Named Bob" by James Bowen is a memoir about a man who befriends a stray cat and how the cat helps him turn his life around.
- ❖ "The Silent Miaow" by Paul Gallico is a book that was written from the perspective of a cat and offers humorous insights into feline behavior.
- ❖ "Cat on a Hot Tin Roof" by Tennessee Williams is a play about a wealthy Southern family and their conflicts, with the title referring to a cat that is stuck on a roof.

TALENTED CATS

- ❖ Didga, an Australian cat, gained fame for her skateboarding skills. With the help of her owner, Robert Dollwet, Didga learned to perform impressive tricks on a skateboard. The talented feline even set a

Guinness World Record in 2016 for the most tricks performed by a cat in one minute.

- In 2013, a cat named Cashnip Kitty became an internet sensation when her owner, Stuart McDaniel, noticed her swiping dollar bills from people passing by their office in Tulsa, Oklahoma. Cashnip Kitty's exploits were posted on social media, and the money she collected was donated to a local homeless shelter.
- Painting: A cat named Morris from Brazil gained fame for his artistic abilities. With a little help from his owner, Morris created abstract paintings using his paws and tail. The artwork was sold to raise funds for animal shelters and rescue organizations.
- Playing musical instruments: Nora, a gray tabby cat from New Jersey, became an internet sensation for her piano-playing abilities. Nora was able to play simple melodies on a piano, and her performances were captured on video and shared online.
- Sailing: Miss Rigby, affectionately known as Rigs, is a cat who lives on a sailboat with her owners. Rigs has been sailing around the world since she was a kitten, and her adventures are documented on social media, inspiring many followers.
- Climbing: Millie, a Utah-based adventure cat, is known for her exceptional rock climbing skills. With her owner, Craig Armstrong, Millie has successfully scaled various rock formations, showcasing her agility and fearlessness.
- Therapy Cat: Oscar, a cat living in a nursing and rehabilitation center in Rhode Island, gained fame for his ability to predict the impending death of patients. Oscar would keep the patients company in their final hours, providing comfort to them and their families.
- Detection Cat: A cat named Mango was trained by her owner to detect peanuts, which could cause a life-threatening allergic reaction in the owner's child. Mango's acute sense of smell allows her to detect even trace amounts of peanuts in food products.
- Tightrope Walking: A talented feline named Russia, also known as the "tightrope-walking cat," gained fame for her incredible balancing skills. Russia can walk across a thin rope, exhibiting grace and precision while doing so.

POPULAR CAT FILMS AND TV SHOWS

- ❖ The famous scene in "The Godfather" where a cat is held by Marlon Brando's character was unplanned and the cat belonged to the film's director, Francis Ford Coppola.

- ❖ The cat who played Mr. Bigglesworth in the Austin Powers movies was actually a sphinx cat named Ted NudeGent.

- ❖ The cat that played Salem in the TV show "Sabrina the Teenage Witch" was played by multiple cats, all of which were trained to perform different tricks and behaviors.

- ❖ The cat that played the title character in the movie "Garfield" was named Crystal and was trained to perform a variety of tricks and behaviors.

- ❖ The cat that played "Church" in the 2019 movie adaptation of Stephen King's "Pet Sematary" was actually played by four different cats, all of which were trained to perform different actions.

- ❖ The cat that played "Mr. Jinx" in the movie "Meet the Parents" was named "Mister" and was trained to perform a variety of tricks and behaviors.

- ❖ The cat that played "Toonces" in the "Saturday Night Live" sketches was named "Smokey" and was trained to ride in a car and perform other stunts.

- ❖ The cat that played "Snowbell" in the movie "Stuart Little" was voiced by actor Nathan Lane.

- The cat that played "Milo" in the movie "The Adventures of Milo and Otis" was actually played by multiple cats, all of which were trained to perform different actions.

ONLINE AND SOCIAL MEDIA CATS

- Lil Bub was a cat with a rare genetic condition that caused her to have a small frame, a tongue that always stuck out, and big, round eyes. She became famous for her cute appearance and was an advocate for animal welfare.

- Maru is a Scottish Fold cat from Japan who became famous for his love of boxes. He has starred in numerous videos and has over 800,000 subscribers on YouTube.

- Nala is a Siamese/Tabby mix who was adopted from a shelter in 2010. Her cute face and expressive eyes have made her a popular Instagram star, with over 4 million followers.

- Socks was a black and white cat who belonged to former U.S. President Bill Clinton and his family. He became famous for his appearances at the White House and was known for his friendly personality.

- Colonel Meow was a Himalayan-Persian crossbreed who held the Guinness World Record for the cat with the longest fur. He had over 350,000 followers on Facebook before his death in 2014.

- Hamilton the Hipster Cat is a tuxedo cat with a distinctive mustache. He has over 800,000 followers on Instagram and is known for his love of adventure.

- Keyboard Cat is a meme that features a video of a cat playing a keyboard. The video has been remixed and parodied numerous times and has become a popular internet sensation.

- Banye is a black and white British Shorthair cat who has a distinct black marking on his face that looks like a mustache. He has over 200,000 followers on Instagram.

- Oskar and Klaus are two cats who became famous for their love of boxes. They have over 10 million views on YouTube and have been featured on numerous TV shows and websites.

- Shironeko, which means "white cat" in Japanese, is a cat that became famous for his love of relaxation. He has been featured in numerous photos and videos and has become a popular meme.
- Snoopybabe is a Persian cat from China who became famous for his adorable face and fluffy fur. He has over 300,000 followers on Instagram and has been featured in numerous news articles and websites.

FAMOUS HOLLYWOOD CATS

- Jonesy, the resourceful ginger cat, played a key role in Ridley Scott's 1979 sci-fi horror film "Alien." This fearless feline faced off against a terrifying alien creature and became a beloved symbol of survival.
- Orangey was a tabby cat who appeared in several films in the 1950s and 1960s, including "Gigot" and "Breakfast at Tiffany's." He was one of the most successful animal actors of his time, winning two Patsy Awards (the animal equivalent of the Oscars) for his performances in "Rhubarb" and "The Incredible Shrinking Man."
- Tardar Sauce, better known as Grumpy Cat, became an internet sensation in 2012 due to her permanently grumpy expression. She went on to appear in several television shows and movies, including "Grumpy Cat's Worst Christmas Ever." She became a cultural phenomenon and symbol of internet humor, with merchandise, memes, and even a coffee drink named after her.

- Morris was an orange tabby cat who appeared in several 9Lives cat food commercials in the 1970s and 1980s. He was known for his distinctive meow and charming personality, and helped to popularize the concept of a "spokescat" in advertising.
- Felix the Cat is an animated character who first appeared in silent films in the 1910s. He went on to star in his own television show, comic strips, and merchandise, becoming one of the most recognizable and beloved cartoon cats of all time.
- Salem is a black cat from the television show "Sabrina, the Teenage Witch." He was a popular character on the show, known for his witty remarks and sassy personality.
- Church is a cat from the horror novel "Pet Sematary" by Stephen King. He is a supernatural cat who is resurrected after being buried in a cursed cemetery, and plays a key role in the book's terrifying plot.
- Binx is a black cat from the film "Hocus Pocus." He is a talking cat who helps the film's protagonists defeat a coven of witches, and has become a beloved Halloween icon in the years since the movie's release.
- Jonesy is a cat from the science fiction film "Alien." He is the pet of the crew of the spaceship Nostromo, and plays a pivotal role in the film's plot.
- Bob is a ginger cat who was adopted by a street musician named James Bowen in London. Their story was chronicled in the book "A Street Cat Named Bob" and the subsequent film adaptation, which helped to raise awareness of the issues of homelessness and animal welfare.
- Mr. Bigglesworth, the iconic hairless Sphynx cat, gained fame for his role in the "Austin Powers" film series. His sinister appearance perfectly complemented Dr. Evil, the franchise's nefarious antagonist.
- DC, the charismatic Siamese cat, played a crucial role in the 1965 Disney film "That Darn Cat!" The film's success led to a 1997 remake, solidifying DC's status as a feline Hollywood legend.
- Keanu, the adorable kitten, starred alongside comedians Keegan-Michael Key and Jordan Peele in the 2016 action-comedy film "Keanu." This tiny feline hero stole the show and the hearts of moviegoers.
- Cheetah, a Bengal cat, played the role of Raja in the 2000 film "Dungeons & Dragons." Cheetah's unique appearance and exceptional agility captured the essence of the magical character.

- Sassy, a Himalayan cat, starred in the family adventure film "Homeward Bound: The Incredible Journey." Her witty commentary and strong personality showcased the depth of feline character in cinema.
- Taylor Swift, a known cat lover, is the proud owner of several feline companions, including Olivia Benson and Meredith Grey. They often make appearances on her social media, showcasing their luxurious lifestyle.
- The 2001 film "The Cat's Meow" was inspired by the alleged murder of film producer Thomas Ince. In the movie, a black cat named Gerty served as a symbol of bad luck and foreshadowed the tragic events.
- Tonto, an orange tabby, shared the screen with Art Carney in the 1974 film "Harry and Tonto." The heartwarming story of their cross-country journey earned Carney an Academy Award for Best Actor.
- Ulysses, a three-legged orange tabby, co-starred with Oscar-nominated actor Joaquin Phoenix in the 2018 film "You Were Never Really Here." Ulysses' powerful on-screen presence added emotional depth to the gripping story.
- Snowbell, a fluffy white Persian, gained fame as the voice of reason in the family film "Stuart Little." Voiced by actor Nathan Lane, Snowbell's character entertained audiences with his wit and sarcasm.
- Catrick Swayze, the Hollywood cat who starred in movies and TV shows, was adopted from a shelter by producer Bob Compton. He went on to star in several films, including "The Great Cat Detective" and "Cats & Dogs," and became a beloved member of the Hollywood community.
- Smudge, a British shorthair, starred alongside Nicole Kidman in the 2001 psychological thriller "The Others." Smudge's striking appearance and eerie demeanor contributed to the film's chilling atmosphere.

CARTOON CATS

- The character Garfield, known for his love of lasagna, was originally rejected by numerous newspapers for being "too sophisticated" for the comic strip market.
- The character Tom from Tom and Jerry was originally designed to be a dark grey color, but the animators switched to a lighter shade of grey to make him more visible on screen.

- The character Felix the Cat was rumored to have been created by a jazz musician who would draw the character during performances and sell the sketches to audience members.
- The character Sylvester the Cat, who is always trying to catch Tweety Bird, has been criticized for promoting violence against animals and perpetuating harmful stereotypes about cats.
- The character CatDog from the Nickelodeon animated series has been the subject of controversy due to his unconventional appearance and the fact that he has both feline and canine traits.
- The character CatDog from the Nickelodeon animated series was inspired by a drawing made by the creator's 4-year-old son, which featured a creature with a cat head on one end and a dog head on the other.
- The character Tom from "Tom and Jerry" was initially named "Jasper" in the series' earliest appearances.
- The character Mr. Mistoffelees from the musical "Cats" has been criticized for perpetuating negative stereotypes about magic and mysticism.
- The character Top Cat from the Hanna-Barbera animated series has been accused of promoting negative stereotypes about cats, portraying them as lazy and unproductive members of society.
- The character Tom from Tom and Jerry has been the subject of controversy for his violent behavior, with some critics arguing that the show promotes harmful messages about conflict resolution.
- The character Garfield has been criticized for perpetuating negative stereotypes about overweight cats and promoting unhealthy eating habits.
- The character Felix the Cat has been the subject of numerous conspiracy theories, with some fans suggesting that the character was inspired by occult beliefs or that he has hidden meanings and symbolism.
- Despite being one of the most recognizable characters in the world, Hello Kitty is actually not a cat, but a little girl named Kitty White.

RICHEST CATS IN THE WORLD

- Choupette, the cat who inherited $200 million from Karl Lagerfeld, was known for her luxurious lifestyle, which included private jets, personal chefs, and diamond necklaces.
- Blackie, the British cat who inherited $12.5 million, was originally a stray cat who was adopted by a wealthy antiques dealer named Ben Rea. Rea had no family and left his entire fortune to Blackie and several cat charities upon his death.
- Maria Assunta left her cat, Tomasso, her entire $13 million fortune when she died in 2011.
- Maru, the Japanese cat with over 600,000 Instagram followers, became famous for his love of boxes and his playful antics. He has starred in multiple viral videos and even has his own book and merchandise line.
- Bagheera, the Russian cat who posed with stacks of cash, was actually part of a photoshoot for a bank's ad campaign. The photos went viral and sparked rumors about the cat's wealth.
- Missy, the American cat with a $500,000 trust fund, was left the money by her owner, a widow who was concerned about the cat's well-being after she passed away. The money is managed by a trustee who ensures that Missy receives top-quality care.
- Prince Chunk, the massive British cat who starred in his own reality TV show, weighed over 40 pounds and became famous after being brought

to a shelter by his owner's family. He went on to become a beloved celebrity and received multiple endorsement deals.

- Tombili, the Turkish cat who became a local celebrity, was known for her love of lounging on the street and striking poses for photos. After her death, a statue was erected in her honor, and she became a symbol of her neighborhood's spirit and love of animals.

- Black, the English cat who inherited $2.5 million, was adopted by the neighbors of his wealthy owner after her death. They had no idea that the cat was so wealthy until they received a letter from her solicitor.

- Princess, the New Zealand cat who received a lifetime achievement award, was known for her philanthropic work and her ability to cheer up people in hospitals and rest homes. Her owner had left her fortune to the SPCA to help care for other animals in need.

- Gigolo, the German cat who inherited over $200,000, was known for his refined taste in food and his love of caviar and lobster.

- Conchita, the socialite cat who inherited $3 million, was known for her fashionable outfits and her appearances on TV shows and in magazines.

- Bart, the Florida cat who dug himself out of his grave, survived the ordeal with minor injuries and went on to become a local celebrity. His inheritance was used to create a fund to help other animals in need.

- Blackberry, the cat who inherited $250,000, was known for her sweet personality and her love of napping in the sun. Her new owner promised to use the money to support animal rescue and adoption efforts.

CAT FOOD SURPRISE

- Certain foods, such as chocolate, onions, and garlic, can be toxic to cats and should be avoided.

- Some cat foods contain synthetic flavors that mimic the taste and smell of prey animals, such as mice and birds, to make them more appealing to cats.

- Cats have a unique sense of taste and may be more sensitive to bitter flavors than humans are.

- Dry food is often marketed as being good for dental health, but there is no scientific evidence to support this claim.

- Some cat foods contain a synthetic version of the amino acid taurine, which is essential for feline health but can be difficult to obtain in sufficient amounts from a natural diet.
- The type of meat used in cat food can impact its nutritional value. For example, chicken is a good source of protein, while fish can be high in mercury and other contaminants.
- Some cats have been known to hunt and eat insects, such as crickets and beetles, as part of their diet.
- Some cats have been known to eat human hair; a condition known as trichophagia. This can lead to hairballs and other digestive issues.

CAT-FRIENDLY BAKERIES

- In 2020, a woman in England created a bakery that specializes in treats and cakes for cats. The bakery, called Lady Dinah's Cat Emporium, offers a range of feline-friendly desserts, including catnip-infused cakes and tuna cookies.
- A cookbook called "Cooking for Two: Your Cat & You" was published in 2017, featuring recipes for homemade cat food and treats that are designed to be shared with the cat's owner.
- In 2019, a man in Japan opened a restaurant that serves meals for both cats and their owners. The restaurant, called Nekoya, offers a range of cat-friendly dishes, such as chicken and fish with added vitamins and minerals, and also allows customers to bring their own cats.

- In 2018, a bakery in New York City called Little Lions created a line of cat-themed desserts, including cupcakes and macarons shaped like cats.
- A Kickstarter campaign launched in 2014 to fund the creation of a cat-shaped cake pan, which would allow cat owners to bake their own feline-themed desserts at home.
- In 2015, a cat cafe in London called Lady Dinah's Cat Emporium hosted a "catio party," where customers could bake and decorate cat-shaped cookies while interacting with the cafe's resident cats.
- In 2016, a cat-themed bakery in Los Angeles called Crumbs & Whiskers launched a line of catnip-infused cupcakes, which quickly became a hit with cat owners.
- A cat cafe in Oakland, California called Cat Town Cafe created a line of cat-themed cocktails, including a "Kitty Colada" and a "Meowgarita," which are served alongside cat-themed desserts like cat-shaped cookies and cupcakes.
- In 2019, a cat cafe in Edinburgh, Scotland called Maison de Moggy began offering baking classes for customers, where they can learn to make cat-themed desserts while interacting with the cafe's resident cats.

FELINE FASHION AND STYLE

- In 2016, a French fashion designer named Jean-Charles de Castelbajac created a line of clothing inspired by his cat, Minou. The collection included pieces like a coat with a cat face on the back and a sweater with a cat-shaped pocket.
- A company called United Bamboo has been creating an annual calendar featuring cats wearing miniature versions of the latest fashion trends since 2010.
- In 2019, a company called Popy Moreni released a line of luxury handbags that are shaped like cats.
- A company called Moshiqa produces luxury pet accessories, including collars, leashes, and beds, that are made with high-end materials like Italian leather and Swarovski crystals.
- In 2015, a cat named Princess Monster Truck became an internet sensation after her unique appearance - a severe underbite and wild fur - caught the attention of fans on social media. Princess Monster Truck has

since become a fashion icon, with fans creating clothing and accessories inspired by her.

- A company called United Nude creates cat-themed shoes, including a pair of kitten heels with cat ears and a tail.

CAT-FRIENDLY DESTINATIONS

- National parks aren't just for dogs - cats can enjoy the great outdoors too! With stunning natural vistas and abundant wildlife, national parks provide a unique adventure for you and your feline companion. Imagine exploring the wilderness with your cat by your side, feeling the fresh air and soaking up the beauty of nature.
- Who says cats don't like the beach? With their love for sunbathing and lounging, cats can enjoy some fun in the sun on pet-friendly beaches..
- Want to pamper your cat on vacation? Many hotels now offer pet-friendly accommodations, including luxurious amenities such as plush pet beds, room service for pets, and even in-room massages for your furry friend! Imagine your cat relaxing in style while you enjoy room service and a bubble bath.
- Camping with your cat? Why not! With pet-friendly campgrounds popping up across the country, camping can be a fun and adventurous activity for you and your feline friend. Imagine roasting marshmallows over the campfire while your cat lounges in their cozy tent, gazing up at the stars.
- Wine tasting with your cat? Yes, it's a thing! Some vineyards allow pets, including cats, to roam their beautiful grounds. Imagine sipping on a glass of wine while your feline friend explores the vineyard, chasing butterflies and enjoying the fresh air.
- Museums and art galleries aren't just for humans - cats can enjoy them too! Some museums and galleries allow pets on leashes, providing a unique and enriching experience for both you and your feline friend. Imagine admiring a beautiful painting with your cat by your side, enjoying the peaceful atmosphere.
- Pet-friendly attractions such as the Monterey Bay Aquarium, the Bronx Zoo, and the Houston Zoo offer a fun and educational experience for both you and your cat. Imagine exploring the wonders of the animal

kingdom with your feline friend, watching them marvel at the exotic creatures and maybe even making a new animal friend or two!

CAT ADVENTURERS

- In 2018, a man named Dean Nicholson quit his job and started cycling around the world. During his travels, he found a stray kitten in Bosnia and Herzegovina and decided to adopt her. Now, Dean and his cat, Nala, have cycled over 12,000 miles together and have become internet sensations.

- A cat named Millie became famous for her love of kayaking with her owner, Craig Armstrong. The pair would often paddle around the waters of Bainbridge Island in Washington State, with Millie perched on the front of the kayak wearing a life jacket. Millie sadly passed away in 2019, but her legacy lives on through her adventures with Craig.

- In 2014, a hiker named Kyle Rohrig set out to hike the entire Appalachian Trail with his cat, Nola. The pair hiked over 2,100 miles together and became the first known cat and owner duo to complete the trail.

- A cat named Jasper has become a beloved resident of a hostel in the Swiss Alps. Jasper is known for his love of hiking and will often accompany hostel guests on hikes through the stunning mountain scenery.

- In 2020, a cat named Viktor became the first cat to reach the summit of Mount Triglav in Slovenia. The mountain is the highest peak in the country, and Viktor's owner, Jana, carried him in a backpack to the top.

- A cat named Honeybee has become a famous feline climber, scaling the walls of her owner's climbing gym in South Africa. Honeybee is known for her agility and fearlessness, and her owner says she is a natural at climbing.

- In 2017, a woman named Mary Irwin set out on a backpacking trip through the Sierra Nevada mountains with her cat, Sophie. The pair hiked over 200 miles together and became the first known cat and owner duo to complete the John Muir Trail.

- A cat named Suki has become an Instagram sensation for her stunning photos of outdoor adventures in Canada. Suki is known for her love of hiking, camping, and exploring the great outdoors with her owner, Martina.

- A cat named Mango has become a beloved figure in the hiking community in California. Mango accompanies her owner, Jen, on hikes throughout the state, and has become known for her adorable hiking gear and her love of exploring new trails.
- A cat named Burrito has become a famous feline rock climber in Thailand. Burrito's owner, Pierre, is a rock climber and often takes his furry friend along on his climbing adventures. Burrito is known for his bravery and love of adventure.

SUPERSTITIONS AND FOLKLORE

- In ancient Egypt, cats were worshiped as gods and killing a cat was punishable by death. Cats were often mummified and buried with their owners.
- In medieval Europe, it was believed that black cats were witches in disguise, and that they brought bad luck. This belief was particularly prevalent during the witch hunts of the 16th and 17th centuries.
- According to Japanese folklore, cats have the power to see ghosts and spirits. This belief is rooted in Shinto and Buddhist traditions and is still widely held today.
- In some cultures, it is believed that if a cat licks a person's hair, it is a sign of good luck. This superstition is particularly prevalent in Asia.
- In some parts of the world, it is believed that if a cat washes behind its ears, it means that rain is coming. This belief is particularly common in parts of the Caribbean and South America.
- In Russian folklore, it is believed that if a cat walks over a person's face while they are sleeping, it is a sign that they will die soon. This belief has been traced back to ancient Slavic traditions.
- In some cultures, it is believed that a cat can predict the weather. If a cat sits with its back to the fire, it means that it will be cold and rainy. This belief is particularly common in parts of Europe.
- In ancient Rome, it was believed that if a cat sneezed during a wedding ceremony, it was a sign of good luck for the couple. This belief has its roots in Roman mythology and is still sometimes referenced today.
- In some African cultures, it is believed that if a cat rubs against a person's legs, it means that they are about to receive money or other good

fortune. This belief is particularly common in parts of West and Central Africa.
- In many cultures, it is believed that cats have nine lives. This belief dates back to ancient Egyptian mythology, which held that cats had the ability to regenerate themselves after death.

MYSTERIOUS BREEDS AND PHENOMENA

- The Sokoke is a cat breed known for its unique, striped coat and originates from Kenya. Despite its striking appearance, little is known about its origins and how it came to be.
- The Aegean is a cat breed that originates from Greece and is known for its muscular body and short, fluffy coat. Despite being an ancient breed, its early history is shrouded in mystery.
- The Singapura is one of the smallest cat breeds and has a unique ticked coat pattern. It originated in Singapore, but little is known about its history and how it came to be.
- The Chartreux is a cat breed known for its plush, blue-gray coat and quiet, reserved personality. It is believed to have originated in France, but little is known about its early history.
- The Japanese Bobtail has a distinctive bobtail and is believed to have been around for centuries. However, little is known about its origins and how it came to be in Japan.
- The Turkish Van is known for its unique, semi-longhair coat and love of water. Its origins are somewhat mysterious, with some believing that it may have originated in central Asia.
- The Serengeti is a hybrid cat breed created to resemble the wild serval cat. Its origins can be traced back to the United States in the 1990s.
- The German Rex is known for its curly, wavy coat and friendly personality. Its origins are somewhat mysterious, with some people believing that it may have been created through a natural genetic mutation.
- The Nebelung is known for its long, silky blue-gray coat and bright green eyes. It is a relatively new breed that was created in the United States in the 1980s.

- The Korat is known for its short, silver-blue coat and playful personality. It originated in Thailand, but little is known about its history before the 1950s.
- The Peterbald is a breed that originated in Russia and is known for its hairless or partially hairless coat. Its origins are somewhat mysterious, with some people believing that it may have been created through a cross between a Siamese and a Donskoy cat.
- The Bengal is known for its striking coat, which resembles that of a wild leopard or tiger. Its origins can be traced back to a domestic cat and an Asian leopard cat crossbreed.
- The Toyger was created to resemble a miniature tiger and is known for its distinctive striped coat. Its origins can be traced back to a Bengal cat and a striped domestic shorthair crossbreed.
- The LaPerm is known for its curly coat and friendly, affectionate nature. Its origins are somewhat mysterious, with some people believing that it may have been created through a natural genetic mutation.
- The Australian Mist is a relatively new breed created in Australia in the 1970s through a crossbreeding program. It is known for its spotted coat and friendly personality.

PERPLEXING CAT PERSONALITY TRAITS

- A study found that cats may be more attracted to people who ignore them, possibly due to their independent nature.
- A survey found that some cats prefer listening to classical music over other genres, such as heavy metal or pop.
- Some cats just love to be strange, and will insist on playing with their water dish or sleeping in unusual places, like a bathtub or kitchen sink.
- Cats are notorious for their love of sitting in boxes, even if they are too small or uncomfortable for them.
- Pica: A behavior in which cats eat non-food items, such as plants, paper, or cloth, often as a result of boredom, stress, or a dietary deficiency.
- Licking plastic: A behavior in which cats lick plastic objects, such as bags or containers, often due to the texture or scent of the plastic.

CATS AROUND THE WORLD

- ❖ The city of Rome, Italy has a population of feral cats that are protected by law and cared for by volunteers.
- ❖ According to a survey conducted in 2019, the United States has the highest cat population in the world, with around 95 million cats living in households. An estimated 500 million cats live in households worldwide.
- ❖ In the United Kingdom, cats are the second most popular pet after dogs, with around 10 million cats living in households.
- ❖ Outdoor domestic cats can have a negative impact on wildlife, as they often hunt small mammals, birds, and reptiles.
- ❖ The average lifespan of an indoor cat is around 15 years, while the lifespan of an outdoor cat is around 2-5 years.
- ❖ Japan is known for its love of cats, and has numerous cat cafes where people can go to interact with cats and enjoy cat-themed treats.
- ❖ The city of Istanbul, Turkey is known for its large population of stray cats, which are beloved by locals and tourists alike.

THREATS TO WILD CAT POPULATIONS

- ❖ The biggest threat to wild cat populations is habitat loss due to deforestation, mining, and human development.

- Wild cats, such as tigers and lions, are often poached for their skin and body parts, which are used in traditional medicine.
- The Iberian Lynx is the most endangered wild cat species in the world, with only around 400 individuals left in the wild.
- Domestic cats are also a threat to wild cat populations, as they can transmit diseases and compete with wild cats for resources.
- The Scottish Wildcat is one of the rarest wild cat species in the world, with only around 35 individuals left in the wild.
- Jaguars are threatened by the illegal wildlife trade, as well as habitat loss due to logging and agriculture.
- Snow Leopards are threatened by climate change, as warming temperatures are causing their habitat to shrink.
- Lions in Africa are threatened by the loss of prey animals due to overhunting and habitat loss.
- Cheetahs are threatened by habitat loss, as well as being hunted by farmers who see them as a threat to their livestock.
- The Florida Panther is one of the rarest wild cat species in the world, with only around 200 individuals left in the wild.
- Wild cats are also threatened by roadkill, as roads often cut through their habitat and make it difficult for them to move around.
- The Asiatic Cheetah is one of the most critically endangered wild cat species in the world, with only around 50 individuals left in the wild.
- The African Golden Cat is threatened by habitat loss due to logging and agriculture, as well as being hunted for its fur.
- Ocelots are threatened by habitat loss due to deforestation, as well as being hunted for their fur.
- The Chinese Mountain Cat is one of the most elusive wild cat species in the world, and little is known about its population status.

PROTECTING OUR FELINE FRIENDS

- The Snow Leopard Trust, an organization dedicated to protecting the endangered snow leopard, employs local herders in Central Asia to monitor and protect snow leopard populations.

- In Australia, the government has launched a program called "Cats to Go" to reduce the impact of feral and outdoor cats on wildlife.
- The Cheetah Conservation Fund in Namibia has developed a program to train Anatolian shepherd dogs to protect livestock and reduce human-wildlife conflict, which is a major threat to cheetah populations.
- The Big Cat Sanctuary in Kent, England provides a home for rescued big cats, including tigers, lions, and leopards, and supports conservation efforts in the wild.
- The Wildcat Haven project in Scotland is working to reintroduce Scottish wildcats to the wild and protect them from hybridization with domestic cats.
- The African Lion and Environmental Research Trust in Zimbabwe uses radio collars to track lion movements and study their behavior, which can help inform conservation efforts.
- The Panthera organization works to protect wild cat populations around the world by partnering with local communities, government agencies, and other conservation groups.
- In Taiwan, a group of cat lovers has built a "cat village" to provide a safe and comfortable home for stray cats.
- The International Fund for Animal Welfare has developed a program to vaccinate domestic cats against diseases that can be transmitted to wild cat populations, such as feline distemper and feline leukemia.
- In India, Project Tiger was launched in 1972 to protect the Bengal tiger and its habitat. The project has helped to increase the tiger population from around 1,200 individuals to over 2,500 today.
- In the United States, the Big Cat Public Safety Act was introduced in 2021 to regulate the ownership and breeding of big cats, such as tigers, lions, and leopards, to prevent animal cruelty and ensure public safety.
- In Japan, there is a program called "Neko Café" which allows people to interact with and play with cats in a café setting. The program helps to provide a safe and comfortable environment for cats, and also provides people with a chance to experience the joys of cat ownership without the long-term commitment.

MY THERAPIST IS A CAT

- ❖ Some cats are trained to be therapy animals, providing emotional support and comfort to people in hospitals, nursing homes, and other care facilities. Therapy cats are carefully selected for their calm and friendly temperament, and they are trained to provide affectionate touch and companionship to people who may be isolated or in need of emotional support.

- ❖ A therapy cat named Oreo was the first cat to be registered as a therapy animal in the United States in 1989. Since then, therapy cats have become increasingly popular as more people recognize the benefits of animal-assisted therapy.

- ❖ Many therapy cats are rescue cats that have been trained and socialized to work with humans. These cats often come from difficult backgrounds and may have been abandoned or abused before they were rescued and trained.

- ❖ Therapy cats can be trained to perform a variety of tasks, such as walking on a leash, riding in a stroller, and wearing a harness. Some therapy cats are even trained to perform tricks or to respond to specific commands.

- ❖ Some therapy cats are specifically trained to work with people with autism, providing a calming presence and helping to reduce anxiety. These cats are often chosen for their gentle temperament and their ability to bond with people with autism.

- A cat named Tara was hailed as a hero in 2014 when she saved a young boy from a dog attack. Following the attack, Tara was trained as a therapy cat and now provides emotional support to children in hospitals.
- A cat named Pusic, who was rescued from the streets of Croatia, has become a social media sensation for his therapy work with children in hospitals. Pusic's story is a testament to the transformative power of animal-assisted therapy and the many ways that animals can bring joy and comfort into our lives.

CAT JOBS

- Service cats can be trained to perform a variety of tasks, such as fetching items, opening doors, or providing tactile stimulation to help calm their owners during anxiety attacks.
- Service cats that are trained to detect seizures can do so by sensing changes in their owner's body language, behavior, or scent. Once a seizure is detected, they may use signals such as meowing or pawing to alert their owner or others, or even activate an emergency alert system.
- Some cats are trained as service animals, assisting people with disabilities such as hearing or visual impairments, seizure disorders, or mobility issues.
- A service cat named Deaf Jeff, who is trained to alert his deaf owner to sounds such as doorbells or smoke alarms, has become a social media sensation for his adorable antics and loving personality.

- A service cat named Honey Bee has gained a large following on social media for her ability to detect changes in her owner's blood sugar levels, alerting her when her blood sugar is too high or too low.
- Service cats are not recognized as official service animals under the Americans with Disabilities Act, which means that they are not guaranteed the same legal protections as service dogs.
- In 2018, a service cat named Mulan made headlines after she helped her owner, a teenager with autism, navigate a crowded airport. The cat was trained to walk on a leash and provide comfort to her owner during stressful situations.
- In 2020, a service cat named Purrscilla became a viral sensation after her owner shared a video of her wearing a backpack and riding on the back of her owner's bicycle. Purrscilla, who is trained to assist her owner with mobility issues, now has thousands of followers on social media.
- In 2017, a service cat named Nala made headlines after she helped her owner, a young girl with a rare genetic disorder, communicate with the world. Nala was trained to respond to her owner's verbal and nonverbal cues, helping her to express her thoughts and feelings in a way that was previously impossible.
- In the United Kingdom, there is a cat named Doorkins Magnificat who serves as the resident cat of Southwark Cathedral in London. Doorkins is known for her friendly demeanor and often greets visitors to the cathedral.
- In the late 1800s, a cat named Tibs became famous for working as a signalman for the South Devon Railway in England. Tibs would sit in the signal box and use his paw to pull levers to control the trains.
- A cat named Felix works as the "Chief Mouser" at Huddersfield Railway Station in England. Felix was hired in 2011 to help keep the station free of rodents and has become a popular celebrity among commuters.
- In Japan, there is a cat named Maru who works as a stationmaster at the Kishi Station. Maru has his own custom-made hat and jacket and is a beloved figure among commuters.
- In the United States, there is a cat named Oreo who works as a library cat at the Sterling Public Library in Massachusetts. Oreo is known for his friendly personality and often sits on patrons' laps as they read.

- A cat named Mr. Peebles works as a receptionist at the offices of the Cat's Protection League in England. Mr. Peebles greets visitors and helps raise awareness about the organization's work.
- In Russia, there is a cat named Zarathustra who works as a philosopher and poet. Zarathustra has written several books and is known for his insightful and humorous observations on life.
- A cat named Palmerston works as the "Chief Mouser" at the Foreign and Commonwealth Office in London. Palmerston is known for his strong personality and has even been involved in some diplomatic incidents with other cats.
- A cat named Max-Arthur works as a piano-playing cat on YouTube. Max-Arthur has become an internet sensation for his musical talents and has even released his own album.
- In Japan, there is a cat named Nyankichi who works as a travel blogger. Nyankichi travels around Japan with his owners and documents his adventures on Instagram and other social media platforms.

FELINE HEALTH IS UNIQUE

- Cats have a unique ability to heal themselves. They produce a purring sound that has a frequency between 25 and 150 Hertz, which has been shown to have therapeutic benefits such as reducing stress, lowering blood pressure, and promoting bone density.
- Cats have fewer taste buds than humans, and they cannot taste sweetness. This is because they are obligate carnivores and their diet consists mainly of meat.
- A cat's normal body temperature is between 100.5 and 102.5 degrees Fahrenheit. That's why they like to snuggle!
- Contrary to popular belief, milk is not good for cats. Most cats are lactose intolerant and cannot digest lactose, a sugar found in milk. Consuming milk can lead to gastrointestinal upset, including vomiting and diarrhea.
- Cats can get heart disease just like humans. Hypertrophic cardiomyopathy (HCM) is the most common form of feline heart disease, and it can lead to heart failure if left untreated.

- ❖ Obesity is a common problem in cats, and it can lead to serious health issues such as diabetes, arthritis, and heart disease. Maintaining a healthy weight through proper diet and exercise is important for your cat's overall health and well-being.

- ❖ Cats can suffer from anxiety and stress, just like humans. Some common causes of feline anxiety include changes in routine, loud noises, separation from their owner, and conflict with other cats. Signs of anxiety in cats may include hiding, excessive grooming, loss of appetite, and aggressive behavior.

- ❖ Cats are tough! They have a strong instinct to hide signs of illness or pain, which can make it difficult for their owners to detect health problems. Regular veterinary checkups and monitoring your cat's behavior for changes can help catch health issues early.

- ❖ Cats have a unique way of conserving water in their bodies. Unlike dogs, cats have a low thirst drive and get most of their water from their food. Feeding your cat wet food can help ensure they are getting enough hydration.

DO YOU LOVE YOUR CAT? THEN DO THIS:

- ❖ Provide them with a view. Cats love to look out of windows and observe their surroundings. Providing your cat with a comfortable perch near a window can help reduce boredom and stress.

- Use pheromone therapy. Pheromone therapy, such as Feliway, can help reduce stress and anxiety in cats. These products mimic the natural pheromones that cats produce to mark their territory and provide a sense of security.
- Incorporate playtime into mealtime. Using puzzle feeders or hiding food around the house can help provide your cat with mental stimulation and exercise during mealtime.
- Use a calming collar. Calming collars, which contain pheromones or herbal extracts, can help reduce stress and anxiety in cats. These collars can be particularly useful for cats that are anxious during travel or visits to the veterinarian.
- Play music. Playing calming music, such as classical music or nature sounds, can help reduce stress and anxiety in cats. It can also help create a relaxing environment for your cat.
- Practice positive reinforcement training. Positive reinforcement training can help reinforce good behavior in cats and reduce unwanted behaviors, such as scratching or biting. This type of training involves rewarding your cat for good behavior with treats or praise.
- Use a water fountain. Cats prefer fresh, running water, and providing them with a water fountain can help encourage them to drink more water and stay hydrated.

CAT ADOPTION STORIES

- A cat named Meatball, who was found wandering the streets in New Jersey, was adopted after her story went viral on social media. Meatball had a unique appearance due to a genetic mutation that caused her eyes to be different colors and her face to be asymmetrical.
- In 2020, a cat named Mr. B was adopted from a shelter in Philadelphia after spending 2,461 days in the shelter. Mr. B became a local celebrity and even had his own Facebook page with over 30,000 followers.
- A woman in Russia adopted a stray cat who turned out to be a rare breed with a value of over $100,000. The cat, named Barsik, had been living on the streets before being taken in by his new owner.
- In 2018, a cat named Symba was adopted from a shelter in Washington D.C. after weighing in at a whopping 35 pounds. Symba went on a weight

loss journey with his new owner and lost over 15 pounds in just six months.

- A cat named Batman was adopted from a shelter in New York City after being rescued from a hoarding situation. Batman had severe dental issues and required extensive surgery, but he made a full recovery and now enjoys life with his new family.

- A cat named Lazarus was adopted from a shelter in Michigan after being found abandoned in a dumpster. Lazarus had suffered from frostbite and required multiple surgeries, but he made a full recovery and now lives a happy life with his new family.

- A woman in Texas adopted a cat named Duchess who had been diagnosed with feline leukemia. Despite the diagnosis, Duchess has lived a happy and healthy life with her new family for over four years.

- In the United States, approximately 3.2 million cats enter animal shelters each year. This means that there are many cats in need of loving homes and adoption can make a huge difference in their lives.

- Adopting a cat from a shelter can be more affordable than buying a cat from a breeder. Adoption fees usually cover the cost of spay/neuter surgery, vaccinations, and other medical care, making it a more cost-effective option.

AWWWW...

- In 2018, a cat named Stormy was rescued from a storm drain in Florida after being trapped for over a week. Stormy required veterinary care but made a full recovery and was eventually adopted.

- A cat named Sir Stuffington was rescued from a hoarding situation in Oregon and became an internet sensation due to his unique appearance, which included a missing eye and scars on his face.

- In 2020, a group of firefighters in California rescued a cat named Baby from a burning building. Baby required oxygen and veterinary care but made a full recovery and was reunited with her owner.

- In 2019, a shelter in Indiana hosted a sleepover event, where visitors could spend the night with cats in the shelter. The event was a success and helped many cats find their forever homes.

- A cat named Homer was rescued from a shelter in California after being deemed "unadoptable" due to his FIV-positive status. Homer went on to become a therapy cat and helped many people in need.
- A cat named Kali was rescued from a shelter in Illinois after being found in a garbage can. Kali required surgery for an injured leg but made a full recovery and was eventually adopted.
- In 2019, a shelter in California hosted a kitten yoga event, where visitors could do yoga while playing with adoptable kittens. The event was a hit and helped many kittens find their forever homes.
- A cat named Willow was rescued from a shelter in Pennsylvania and went on to become a social media sensation due to her unique appearance, which included an underbite and crossed eyes.
- In 2018, a cat named Sully was rescued from a drainpipe in Texas after being trapped for three days. Sully required veterinary care but made a full recovery and was eventually adopted.
- A shelter in Florida hosts an annual "Kitten Bowl" event, where visitors can watch adoptable kittens play football on a miniature field. The event helps raise awareness for cat adoption and has helped many kittens find their forever homes.
- In 2019, a cat named Rubble was rescued from a shelter in the UK and became the oldest living cat in the world at the age of 31. Rubble passed away later that year, but his story inspired many cat lovers around the world.
- A cat named Thor was rescued from a shelter in Utah and went on to become a "spokes-cat" for a local pet food company. Thor's unique appearance and outgoing personality made him a hit with pet owners.
- In 2020, a shelter in Canada hosted a "speed dating" event, where visitors could meet adoptable cats in a speed dating format. The event helped many cats find their forever homes and was a fun and unique way to promote cat adoption.
- In 2019, a kitten named Tiny was rescued from a storm drain in California. Tiny had fallen into the drain and was unable to get out on her own. Firefighters used a special camera to locate Tiny and safely retrieve her from the drain.

HOME IS WHERE THE CAT IS

- ❖ Cats have a strong sense of territory and view their home as their own personal kingdom. A cat's home is where they feel the most comfortable and secure, and it serves as their base for exploring and interacting with the world around them.
- ❖ A cat's perception of their home is largely based on their sense of smell, which is much stronger than that of humans. Cats use their sense of smell to recognize familiar scents and mark their territory by rubbing their scent glands on objects in their home.
- ❖ A cat's home serves as a safe haven where they can rest and relax without feeling threatened. A cat's home provides them with a sense of security and a place where they can retreat to when they feel stressed or anxious.
- ❖ Cats often mark their territory by rubbing their scent glands on objects in their home, such as furniture and toys. This behavior helps to establish their ownership of their home and create a sense of familiarity and security.
- ❖ A cat's perception of their home can be influenced by the presence of other pets or people. Cats may view their home as a shared space and may feel threatened or uncomfortable if they perceive other pets or people as invading their territory.
- ❖ Cats may become stressed if their home environment changes suddenly, such as if furniture is moved or if new pets or people are introduced. This

is because cats thrive on routine and familiarity, and sudden changes can disrupt their sense of security and well-being.

- Cats are highly adaptable and can adjust to changes in their home environment over time. While sudden changes can be stressful, cats are capable of adapting to new situations and can eventually become comfortable with new people, pets, or changes in their surroundings.
- A cat's home provides them with opportunities for play and exploration, which are important for their physical and mental health. Cats need access to toys, scratching posts, and other objects that allow them to engage in natural behaviors such as hunting, scratching, and climbing.
- Cats may become attached to specific objects in their home, such as a favorite toy or a cozy bed. These objects provide cats with a sense of comfort and security and can become important parts of their daily routines.
- A cat's perception of their home can have a significant impact on their behavior and overall well-being. Providing a safe and stimulating environment is important for a cat's health and happiness, and can help prevent stress-related health problems such as urinary tract infections and behavior issues like aggression and anxiety.
- Studies have found that cats have a preference for certain colors in their home environment. Cats are attracted to colors in the blue-violet range, which may be why many cat toys and beds are colored blue or purple.
- Research has found that cats are sensitive to changes in the lighting and temperature of their home environment. Cats may prefer areas of their home that are cooler or warmer, and may seek out areas with natural light or warm spots near radiators or windows.
- Cats are highly sensitive to the quality of the air in their home environment. Poor air quality can cause respiratory issues in cats and may lead to stress and anxiety.
- Studies have shown that cats are highly sensitive to sounds in their home environment, including low-frequency vibrations that humans may not be able to hear. Cats may be particularly sensitive to sounds associated with prey, such as rustling or scratching.
- Research has found that cats may be more likely to exhibit territorial behavior when they are in a stressful or unfamiliar situation. For example, cats may be more likely to mark their territory when they are introduced to a new pet or person.

- Cats may be more likely to exhibit territorial behavior when they are in pain or feeling unwell. This may be a form of resource guarding, as the cat seeks to protect their territory and resources.

WHY DID MY CAT SPRAY MY CHAIR?

- Territoriality is a natural behavior for cats and helps them establish and maintain a sense of ownership over their surroundings.
- Territoriality can help reduce stress and anxiety in cats, as it provides them with a sense of security and familiarity.
- A cat's territorial behavior is linked to their hunting instincts, as they use their sense of smell and marking behavior to identify and track prey.
- Territorial behavior can also serve as a communication tool for cats, as they use their scent markings to communicate with other cats in their territory.
- Encouraging play and physical activity can help reduce territorial behavior, as cats will have an outlet for their energy and natural hunting instincts.
- Providing cats with designated spaces, such as scratching posts and cozy beds, can also help promote territorial behavior in a positive way, by giving cats a sense of ownership and security over their surroundings.
- Maintaining a consistent routine and environment can also help reduce territorial behavior, as cats thrive on predictability and familiarity.

- Some cats may exhibit territorial behavior towards outdoor objects, such as trees or bushes, in addition to objects inside the home. This can indicate a need for more outdoor space or a desire for exploration and stimulation.
- Cats who are confined to small spaces, such as indoor cats, may exhibit territorial behavior more frequently, as they feel a need to establish their presence in a limited environment.
- Female cats can be just as territorial as males, especially if they are not spayed. Female cats may mark their territory with urine, and can become aggressive towards other cats who enter their territory.

MOST COMMON CAT NAMES

- In Japan, the most popular cat name is Tama, which means "jewel" or "ball" in Japanese. This name has become popular because of a famous cat named Tama, who served as the stationmaster at a train station in Wakayama Prefecture. Tama became a local celebrity and was credited with boosting tourism to the area.
- In Spain, the most popular cat name is Luna, which means "moon" in Spanish. This name is popular because of its beautiful sound and its association with the night sky and the mystical.
- In Russia, the most popular cat name is Murka, which means "little cat" in Russian. This name is popular because it is a diminutive form of the word "cat" in Russian, and it is also a term of endearment for a small, cute cat.
- In France, the most popular cat name is Minou, which means "kitty" in French. This name is popular because it is a cute and affectionate nickname for a cat, and it has a classic French sound.
- In the United States, the most popular cat names are Bella and Max. These names are popular because they are short, easy to pronounce, and they sound friendly and approachable.
- In Thailand, the most popular cat name is Maeow, which is the Thai word for "meow." Not very original, is it? Meow!
- In Italy, the most popular cat name is Gatto, which means "cat" in Italian.

- In Sweden, the most popular cat name is Socks, which refers to the cat's paws. This name is popular because it is a cute and playful name that reflects the cat's adorable features.
- In the United Kingdom, the most popular cat name is Charlie. This name is popular because it is a classic and friendly name that works well for both male and female cats.
- In Brazil, the most popular cat name is Chico. This name is popular because it is a cute and playful name that is easy to pronounce and remember. It also has a friendly and approachable sound that works well for cats.

SOME FUN CAT NAMES

- Professor Purrfect: A name that speaks to the cat's intelligence and playfulness, this title is purrfect for a feline who always seems to have the answers.
- Sir Reginald Fluffybutt: This royal moniker perfectly captures the regal appearance and fluffy tail of this majestic feline. Who wouldn't want to bow down to a fluffy butt-ed Sir?
- Meowingtons: A playful name that incorporates the cat's love of making noise, Meowingtons is a nod to the cat's mischievous nature. You'll never run out of entertainment with a cat named Meowingtons!

- Chairman Meow: This name references the cat's leadership qualities and love of napping, making it the perfect choice for a cat who runs the household with an iron paw...when they're not napping, of course.
- Admiral Snuggles: Celebrating the cat's cuddly and affectionate personality, this name is perfect for a feline who loves to snuggle. Who wouldn't want to sail the high seas with a snuggly admiral?
- Sir Whiskerface: This name is a nod to the cat's impressive whiskers and is a celebration of the feline's unique and distinguished features.
- Duchess Furrball: This regal name emphasizes the cat's luxurious appearance, making it the purrfect choice for a feline who always looks and feels fabulous!
- Lady Pawsington: This delicate and graceful name references the cat's graceful movements, making it a great choice for a feline who always walks with poise.
- Baron von Scratchy: This playful and mischievous name celebrates the cat's love of play and its tendency to get into trouble!

CAT-RELATED HOLIDAYS AND FESTIVALS

- The Amsterdam Cat Festival is an annual event that celebrates all things feline. It features a range of cat-related attractions, from cat-themed markets to cat cafes, and even a cat adoption boat ride along Amsterdam's canals.

- The CatCon festival in the US is an annual two-day event that is held in Los Angeles, California. It features a range of cat-related attractions, from celebrity guest appearances to workshops on cat health and behavior.

- The Cat Video Festival in Minneapolis is an annual event that was created in 2012 by the Walker Art Center. It has since become one of the largest celebrations of cat videos in the world, attracting thousands of attendees each year.

- The Cat Cafe trend started in Japan, where cat cafes have been popular for many years. The concept has since spread to countries around the world, including the US, Canada, and Europe.

- The Cat Art Show in Los Angeles is an annual event that showcases a range of cat-inspired artwork from both established and emerging artists. The event has been running since 2014 and has featured the work of over 100 artists.

- The International Cat Video Festival is a touring festival that has been hosted in countries around the world, from Japan to Australia. The festival features a selection of the best cat videos from around the world, as well as cat-related events and activities.

- The Kattenstoet festival in Belgium is held every three years in the city of Ypres. It is a celebration of cats and features a parade of cat-themed floats, music, and costumes.

- The Cat Video Festival in Minneapolis has screened over 100 cat videos since its inception, and has featured a range of viral sensations such as Keyboard Cat and Henri, le Chat Noir.

- Feline Good Cat Festival in Malaysia: This festival is held in Kuala Lumpur and features a range of cat-related attractions, including cat adoptions, cat-themed workshops, and even a cat-themed cafe.

- Cat Carnival in Singapore: This annual event is held at the Singapore Expo and features a range of cat-related activities, including cat shows, cat adoptions, and even a cat cafe.

- Cat Festival in Thailand: This festival is held in various cities across Thailand, including Bangkok, and features a range of cat-related attractions, such as cat shows, cat-themed merchandise, and even a cat beauty pageant.

CAT HOLIDAYS, CAT FOODS

- In Japan, there is a holiday called "Cat Day" where people traditionally eat fish-shaped cakes called "maneki neko" or "beckoning cat" cakes.

- In Mexico, on Dia de los Muertos, it is common to prepare cat-shaped candies made of sugar and chocolate called "calaveritas de gato" as an offering to deceased cats.

- Some cat owners prepare special homemade treats for their cats during the holidays, such as turkey or chicken-flavored cat food, catnip cookies, or tuna cakes.

- During Christmas, some cat owners give their cats a small piece of cooked turkey or chicken as a special treat.

- In Italy, there is a holiday called "La Festa dei Gatti" or "The Festival of Cats" where people traditionally eat foods shaped like cats, such as pasta in the shape of a cat's head or a cake in the shape of a cat's face.

- In some cultures, it is believed that certain foods can bring good luck or fortune to cats, such as fish or seafood. During the Chinese New Year, for example, some cat owners feed their cats fish as a symbol of prosperity.

- In Scotland, some cat owners prepare a special dish called "Cullen skink" that is made with smoked haddock and potatoes as a treat for their cats.

- In Japan, there is a traditional New Year's dish called "osechi ryori" that is served in special bento boxes and often includes foods that are considered lucky or auspicious for the coming year, such as shrimp or black beans. Some cat owners may also prepare a special "osechi" for their cats during the New Year.

- During Halloween, some cat owners may give their cats a small piece of pumpkin as a special treat, as pumpkin is known to help regulate digestion and prevent hairballs.

CAT-RELATED CHARITY EVENTS

- ❖ The Kitten Bowl is an annual event that airs on the Hallmark Channel and features adoptable kittens playing football. The event raises awareness about pet adoption and raises money for animal rescue organizations.

- ❖ The Best Friends National Conference is an annual event that brings together animal welfare professionals and advocates from around the world to share ideas and strategies for saving the lives of cats and other animals.

- ❖ The Feline Follies is an annual event in New York City that showcases the talents of cats and their human companions. The event raises money for animal rescue organizations.

- ❖ The Black Cat Ball is an annual event in Seattle, Washington, that raises money for local animal rescue groups and features a silent auction, live music, and a cat costume contest.

- ❖ The Great Catsby Cat Art Show is an annual event in Los Angeles, California, that showcases art inspired by cats and raises money for local animal welfare organizations.

- ❖ The Feline Film Festival is an annual event in Santa Fe, New Mexico, that showcases short films about cats and their human companions. The event raises money for animal rescue organizations.

- ❖ The Catsbury Park Cat Convention is an annual event in Asbury Park, New Jersey, that celebrates cats and raises money for local animal rescue organizations. The event features celebrity guests, adoptable cats, and cat-themed vendors.

- The Feline Good Social Club is a cat café in Denver, Colorado, that hosts regular events and fundraisers for local animal rescue organizations. The café also partners with local businesses to provide discounts to customers who donate to animal rescue groups.

- The Architects for Animals Giving Shelter event is an annual charity event in Los Angeles, California, where architects and designers create unique outdoor shelters for cats, which are then auctioned off to raise money for local animal rescue organizations.

- The Cat Welfare Association in Singapore organizes an annual "Cats Napping Day" event where participants take a nap with adoptable cats to raise awareness about the importance of providing cats with a comfortable and safe space to rest.

- The Alley Cat Allies National Cat Conference is an annual event that brings together advocates for feral and community cats to share strategies and ideas for improving the lives of outdoor cats. The event raises awareness about the importance of Trap-Neuter-Return (TNR) programs.

CAT BURGLARS

- Bill Mason, known as "The Gentleman Thief," stole millions of dollars' worth of jewelry and valuables in the 1960s and 1970s. He was so skilled at his craft that he eluded police for years before finally being caught and serving time in prison.

- Charles "The Ghost" Kennedy gained notoriety as a cat burglar in the 1950s and 1960s in the US. He burglarized the homes of celebrities like Tyrone Power and Zsa Zsa Gabor, stealing millions in jewelry and other valuables.

- The Pink Panthers, an international network of jewel thieves, have pulled off daring heists since the 1990s. They got their name after British police found a stolen diamond ring hidden in a jar of face cream, reminiscent of a scene from the 1963 film "The Pink Panther."

- Peter Scott, dubbed the "King of the Cat Burglars," was a British thief who targeted the wealthy and famous in the 1960s and 1970s. He infamously stole a Picasso painting and jewelry from Sophia Loren.

- Doris Payne, an international jewel thief, has a criminal career spanning six decades. She's stolen millions of dollars' worth of jewelry around the world, using her charm and wit to outsmart security and sales staff.
- Vjeran Tomic, known as the "Spider-Man" burglar, gained fame for his acrobatic heists in Paris. In 2010, he stole five valuable paintings from the Musée d'Art Moderne de la Ville de Paris by scaling the building.
- Blane David Nordahl, nicknamed the "Burglar to the Stars," targeted wealthy homeowners in the US during the 1980s and 1990s. His focus was on high-end silverware, and he reportedly stole over $3 million worth of items.
- John "Spider" Wilson was a British cat burglar who targeted the rich and famous in the 1970s and 1980s. His exploits included stealing jewelry from the film star Joan Collins.
- Ignacio "Nacho" Coronel Villarreal, a Mexican drug lord, was also known as "El Gato" (The Cat) due to his ability to evade law enforcement for years. While not a traditional cat burglar, his nickname reflected his elusive nature.
- The "Basil" burglar, still unidentified, played a key role in the infamous 2015 Hatton Garden heist in London. Basil gained entry by disabling the alarm system and drilling into the vault, stealing millions in cash, jewelry, and other valuables.
- In 2018, a group of cat burglars known as "The Feline Four" were arrested in London, England after a series of high-end jewelry store heists. The Feline Four were known for their coordination and use of cat-like movements and techniques to evade capture.
- In 2016, a notorious cat burglar known as "The Catwoman" was arrested in Los Angeles, California after a series of high-end jewelry store robberies. The Catwoman was known for her use of cat-like movements and techniques, as well as her signature black cat costume and mask.
- In 2015, a group of cat burglars known as "The Cat Pack" were arrested in Miami, Florida after a series of high-end jewelry store heists. The Cat Pack was known for their coordination and use of cat-like movements and techniques, as well as their use of black cat masks to conceal their identities.

REAL CATS THAT WERE THIEVES

- Dusty the Klepto Kitty: Dusty, a domestic cat from San Mateo, California, gained fame for stealing various items from his neighbors. Over the years, Dusty reportedly stole more than 600 items, including shoes, towels, and toys. His thefts were documented on Animal Planet's "Must Love Cats" show.

- Frankie the Cat Burglar: A cat named Frankie, living in Swindon, England, was known for stealing gloves, hats, and other items from nearby homes. His thieving exploits were well-documented by his owner, who started a Facebook group to reunite the stolen items with their rightful owners.

- Brigit the Underwear Thief: A cat named Brigit from Hamilton, New Zealand, gained notoriety for stealing men's underwear and socks from her neighbors. Her owner discovered the stolen items in their home and attempted to return them to the rightful owners.

- Theo the Bra Thief: A cat named Theo from Bristol, England, had a penchant for stealing bras from his neighbors' clotheslines. His owner found a stash of bras in their garden and posted about it on social media to return the stolen items.

- Norris the Slipper Thief: A cat named Norris from Bristol, England, became infamous for stealing slippers from his neighbors. He brought home over 50 pairs of slippers during his crime spree, much to the amusement of his owner.

- Cooper the Toy Thief: Cooper, a cat from Portland, Oregon, made a habit of stealing stuffed animals from his neighbors. His owner discovered a stash of toys that Cooper had collected and returned them to their rightful owners.
- Milly the Clothes Thief: A cat named Milly from Southampton, England, was caught stealing clothes from her neighbors' clotheslines.
- Charlie the Sunglasses Thief: Charlie, a cat from Los Angeles, California, had a penchant for stealing sunglasses. His owner would often find various pairs of sunglasses in their home, presumably taken from unsuspecting neighbors or visitors.
- Maddy the Bag Thief: Maddy, a cat from Sydney, Australia, was known for stealing bags from her neighbors. She would sneak into their homes and snatch bags, bringing them back to her owner as trophies.
- Oliver the Shoe Thief: Oliver, a cat from Pennsylvania, developed a habit of stealing shoes from his neighbors' porches. His owner discovered a collection of over 100 shoes in their yard, all taken by Oliver.
- Esme the Swimsuit Thief: Esme, a cat from Devon, England, was notorious for stealing swimsuits from her neighbors' gardens. Her owner discovered a collection of swimsuits, some still wet from being worn, and attempted to return them to their owners.
- Oscar the Mask Thief: During the COVID-19 pandemic, a cat named Oscar from Portland, Oregon, began stealing face masks from his neighbors. His owner would find various masks around their home and yard, likely taken from neighbors who had hung them out to dry or unattended.
- In 2019, a cat named Boots was caught red-handed stealing items from his neighbors in a small town in England. Boots was known for his mischievous antics and was often seen sneaking into homes and stealing items such as socks, toys, and even jewelry.
- In 2018, a cat named Shadow was caught stealing items from local businesses in a small town in California. Shadow was known for his stealth and was often seen sneaking into stores and stealing small items such as pens, paper clips, and even cash.
- In 2016, a cat named Mittens was caught stealing items from local schools in a small town in New York. Mittens was known for his love of shiny objects and was often seen sneaking into schools and stealing items such as pencils, erasers, and even coins from the school's vending machines.

COLORS AND PATTERNS

- Cats with a "harlequin" pattern have large patches of black and white fur, creating a dramatic and eye-catching look. This pattern is often seen in the Turkish Van cat breed.
- Cats with black coats are less likely to be adopted than cats with other coat colors. This is known as the "black cat bias."
- A cat's fur color and pattern is determined by a variety of factors including genetics, breed, and even temperature.
- Some cats have a "ghost tabby" pattern, which means that they have the gene for tabby markings but they aren't expressed visibly in their coat.
- Calico cats are almost always female. This is because the gene for calico coloring is linked to the X chromosome.
- The Siamese cat breed is known for its "points," which are dark-colored areas on the face, ears, feet, and tail. These points are caused by a temperature-sensitive enzyme that produces darker pigmentation in cooler areas of the body.
- Tortoiseshell cats are known for their unique blend of black, orange, and brown patches. It is said that in ancient times, these cats were believed to bring good luck to their owners.
- Some cats have a "smoke" coloring, which means that the ends of their fur are a lighter color than the roots. This creates a subtle shading effect.

- The Abyssinian cat breed has a unique ticked tabby pattern, which gives their fur a "salt and pepper" appearance.
- Cats with white fur and blue eyes are often deaf. This is because the gene that causes white fur and blue eyes is linked to the gene for deafness.
- Some cats have a "brindle" pattern, which is similar to the pattern seen in some dog breeds. This pattern features thin stripes that are close together, giving the coat a unique, almost marbled appearance.
- The Egyptian Mau cat breed is known for its distinctive "spotted" pattern, which is thought to resemble the markings of wild cats.
- Some cats have a "tabico" pattern, which is a combination of tabby and tortoiseshell coloring. This creates a unique and eye-catching look.
- The color of a cat's nose leather (the skin on their nose) can vary based on their coat color. For example, cats with white fur may have pink nose leather, while cats with black fur may have black nose leather.
- The Manx cat breed is known for its distinctive lack of a tail, but they can also come in a variety of coat colors and patterns.

MORE CAT EXPRESSIONS

- "Cat's eyes" is a term used to describe a type of reflective road stud that is embedded in the road to help drivers navigate in low light conditions.
- The term "catfishing" is used to describe a deceptive online practice where someone creates a fake online identity to deceive or manipulate others.
- "Cattywampus" is a slang term used to describe something that is crooked or askew, and can also mean something that is disorganized or chaotic.
- A "catamaran" is a type of boat that features two parallel hulls, allowing for increased stability and speed.
- The term "catcall" refers to a whistle, shout, or other loud noise made to express disapproval or attract attention, often directed at women in a derogatory manner.

- "Cat's cradle" is a game that is played with string, involving intricate patterns and shapes that are created by looping and weaving the string around the hands and fingers.
- A "catwalk" is a narrow platform that is elevated above the ground, often used in fashion shows to showcase models and their outfits.
- The "cat o' nine tails" is a type of whip that was historically used for corporal punishment in the navy and other institutions.
- A "catbird seat" is a term used to describe a position of power or advantage, often in a business or political context.
- "Cat's paw" is a term used to describe someone who is unwittingly used by another person to carry out their own agenda.
- A "cat's eye" gemstone is a type of chrysoberyl that is known for its chatoyancy, or "cat's eye" effect, where a narrow band of light is reflected in a line across the surface of the stone.
- "Cat's whisker" - used to describe something that is very close or precise, like the fine hairs on a cat's whiskers. This expression is used to describe something that is very accurate or precise, like a measurement that is very close to the exact amount.
- "Feline grace" - used to describe someone who moves with elegance and poise, like a cat. This expression is used to describe someone who moves with a smooth, fluid motion, like a cat walking or jumping.
- "Feline intuition" - used to describe a person's ability to sense or anticipate things, like a cat's heightened senses. This expression is used to describe a person's ability to pick up on subtle cues or anticipate events, like a cat being able to sense danger or prey.
- "Feline humor" - used to describe a type of humor that is subtle and understated, like a cat's playful behavior. This expression is used to describe a type of humor that is characterized by understated wit or irony, like a cat's playful and mischievous behavior.
- "Cat's tongue" - a type of pastry dough that is flaky and crumbly, like a cat's tongue. This expression is used to describe a type of pastry that has a texture similar to a cat's tongue, with a light and flaky crumb.

CAT PROPORTIONS

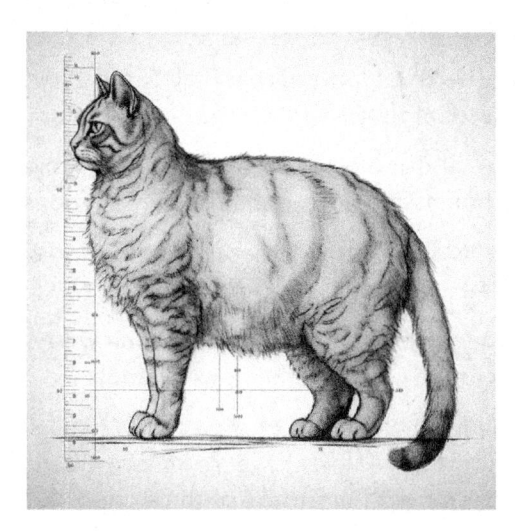

- ❖ The length of a cat's tail is usually equal to the length of their body. However, some breeds like the Manx and Japanese Bobtail have shorter tails or no tails at all.
- ❖ The size of a cat's whiskers is roughly equal to the width of their body. This allows them to navigate through tight spaces without getting stuck.
- ❖ Some cats have an extra fold of skin on their ears, known as ear tufts or lynx tips. This is most commonly seen in breeds like the Maine Coon and the American Bobtail.
- ❖ A cat's eyes are set slightly wider apart than their human counterparts, giving them a wider field of vision and making them excellent hunters.
- ❖ Cats have a specialized collar bone, known as the "clavicle," that allows them to move their front legs independently of each other, giving them more flexibility and agility.
- ❖ The Egyptian Mau cat breed is known for its long, lean body and disproportionately large hind legs, which allow it to run faster than most other cat breeds.
- ❖ Persian cats are known for their flat faces and shortened muzzles, which give them a distinctive "smushed" appearance.
- ❖ The Maine Coon cat breed is known for its large size, with males often weighing up to 18 pounds. Despite their size, they are known for their agility and graceful movements.

- The Balinese cat breed is essentially a long-haired Siamese, with the same triangular head and large ears, but with a longer, more luxurious coat.
- The Scottish Fold cat breed is known for its unique folded ears, which give them a distinctive and cute appearance.
- The Bombay cat breed is known for its sleek, black coat and large, expressive eyes. Despite their somewhat stocky build, they are incredibly agile and athletic.
- The Devon Rex cat breed is known for its large, wide-set ears and curly fur. Despite their somewhat odd appearance, they are friendly and affectionate pets.
- The Singapura cat breed is known for its small size and large, expressive eyes. Despite their diminutive stature, they are known for their energetic and playful personalities.
- The American Shorthair cat breed is known for its sturdy build and balanced proportions. They are often used as the "model" for cat cartoons and illustrations.

INDICATIONS THERE'S A CAT AROUND SOMEWHERE

- A well-worn path or trail in the grass or foliage may indicate a cat's preferred route or territory, as cats are known to follow the same path repeatedly.
- Scratched trees or fence posts can be a sign of a cat's presence, as cats often use these objects to sharpen their claws and mark their territory.
- A patch of flattened or discolored grass may indicate a cat's preferred spot for sunbathing or napping.
- The presence of small paw prints in the dirt or mud can be a clear indication that a cat has been walking or hunting in the area.
- A scratched or damaged birdhouse or other small structure may indicate that a cat has been attempting to access the area in search of prey.
- The presence of feathers, fur, or other small debris in a cat's favorite resting spot may indicate that they have been grooming themselves or shedding.

- The presence of small holes or gaps in a fence or wall may indicate that a cat has been using the area as a means of travel or escape.
- A pungent or musky odor on furniture or other objects may indicate that a cat has been marking its territory with urine or other secretions.
- The presence of small bite marks or puncture wounds on plants or other objects may indicate that a cat has been using them for play or scratching.
- The presence of dead rodents, birds, or insects in the area may indicate that a cat has been hunting or scavenging for food.

CAT LYRICS

- The song "Love Cats" by The Cure includes the lyrics "We move like cagey tigers / We couldn't get closer than this."
- The phrase "cool cats" appears in the lyrics of the classic jazz song "Salt Peanuts" by Dizzy Gillespie and Kenny Clarke.
- The song "Stray Cat Strut" by the Stray Cats includes the lyrics "I don't bother chasing mice around / I slink down the alley looking for a fight."
- The chorus of the song "Everybody Wants to Be a Cat" from the Disney movie "The Aristocats" includes the lyrics "Cause cats are the only cats who know / where it's at."
- The 1990s hit "Black Cat" by Janet Jackson includes the lyrics "I've got nine lives, can't lose / I've been struck by lightning, just like you."

- The classic rock song "Cat Scratch Fever" by Ted Nugent includes the lyrics "I make the pussy purr with the stroke of my hand / They know they're gettin' it from me."

- The song "The Cat's in the Cradle" by Harry Chapin includes the lyrics "My child arrived just the other day / He came to the world in the usual way / But there were planes to catch and bills to pay / He learned to walk while I was away."

- The song "Stray Cat Blues" by the Rolling Stones includes the lyrics "I can see that you're 15 years old / No, I don't want your I.D. / You look so restless and you're so far from home / But it's no hanging matter / It's no capital crime."

- The song "Honky Cat" by Elton John includes the lyrics "When I look back, boy, I must have been green / Boppin' in the country, fishin' in a stream / Lookin' for an answer, tryin' to find a sign / Until I saw your city lights, honey, I was blind."

- The song "Cool for Cats" by Squeeze includes the lyrics "She said the man in the gabardine suit was a spy / I said, 'Be careful, his bowtie is really a camera'."

- The song "Cats and Dogs" by The Head and the Heart includes the lyrics "Well, you know that I love you like a house cat loves a mouse / But sometimes you gotta watch out."

- The song "The Lovecats" by The Cure includes the lyrics "We should have each other to tea, huh? / We should have each other with cream / Then curl up in the fire and sleep for awhile."

- The song "Cat People (Putting Out Fire)" by David Bowie includes the lyrics "See these eyes so green / I can stare for a thousand years / Colder than the moon / Well, it's been so long / And I've been putting out fire with gasoline."

- The song "Kitty" by The Presidents of the United States of America includes the lyrics "I'm gonna shake you off though / Get up on my feet / You're the cutest thing I ever did see / Really love your peaches, want to shake your tree."

- The song "Cat's Eye" by Suzanne Vega includes the lyrics "And the cat's eye / And the pearl / They're just hanging there and making me swirl."

CAT'S PAJAMAS

- Have you ever seen a cat wearing a cowboy hat? Well, it's a sight to behold, partner. These cat-sized hats will make your feline friend look like they just rode in from the Wild West.

- For the most dashing of cats, there are tuxedos made just for them. When they wear one, you can almost hear them saying, "shaken, not stirred."

- Did you know that cats have been spotted sporting bow ties that would make James Bond envious? It's true, these cat-sized accessories add a touch of sophistication and class to any feline wardrobe.

- In the cold months, cats can stay warm and stylish with cat-sized sweaters. Whether they're lounging by the fire or strutting their stuff outside, they'll look good doing it.

- Feline superheroes rejoice! There are cat-sized costumes that will transform your feline friend into their favorite comic book character. Watch out, evil-doers!

- For female felines who want to look their best, there are cat-sized dresses that are perfect for any occasion. From fancy dinners to just lounging around the house, these dresses will make them the belle of the ball.

- When cats want to be comfortable and stylish, they turn to cat-sized hoodies. These are perfect for lazy days spent napping or playing with toys.

- Ahoy, mateys! If your feline friend dreams of being a pirate, there are cat-sized costumes that will make them feel right at home on the high seas.
- For cats who love to dance and twirl, there are cat-sized tutus that will make them the star of the show. They're perfect for birthday parties or just showing off.
- During the holiday season, cats can get in the spirit with cat-sized Santa Claus costumes. They'll be spreading joy and cheer to all they meet.
- What's cooler than a cat-sized leather jacket? Nothing, that's what. If your feline friend is a rebel at heart, this is the perfect accessory for them.
- For cats who want to make a statement, there are cat-sized protest signs that they can wear around their necks. Whether they're fighting for more catnip or a better world for felines, they'll be heard loud and clear.
- If your cat loves the beach, they can now look the part with a cat-sized shark costume. They'll be the talk of the town - or at least the talk of the litter box.
- For felines who want to embrace their inner diva, there are cat-sized sunglasses that will make them look like they're ready for the catwalk. They'll be the coolest cat around.
- Finally, if your cat wants to feel like a queen, there are cat-sized tiaras that will make them feel like royalty. They'll be the envy of all the other cats in the neighborhood.

CAT LIVES MATTER

- In Belgium, it is illegal to own a cat that has not been microchipped, and those who violate this law can face fines of up to €500.
- In Germany, it is illegal to declaw a cat, and those who do can face fines of up to €25,000.
- In Switzerland, it is illegal to keep a single cat, as they are considered social animals, and those who do can face fines of up to 20,000 CHF.
- In Singapore, it is illegal to keep more than three cats in a single household, and those who do can face fines of up to $4,000 SGD.

- In Australia, it is illegal to abandon a cat, and those who do can face fines of up to $33,000 AUD.
- In Israel, it is illegal to abandon a cat, and those who do can face fines of up to 226,000 ILS.
- In Denmark, it is illegal to let a cat roam freely outside, and those who do can face fines of up to 2,500 DKK.
- In Norway, it is illegal to keep a cat indoors for extended periods of time, and those who do can face fines of up to 20,000 NOK.
- In Italy, it is illegal to sell cats under eight weeks old, and those who do can face fines of up to €10,000.
- In France, it is illegal to mistreat a cat, and those who do can face fines of up to €30,000.
- In the United Kingdom, it is illegal to harm or injure a cat, and those who do can face fines of up to £20,000.
- In Spain, it is illegal to mistreat a cat, and those who do can face fines of up to €60,000.
- In Taiwan, it is illegal to sell or consume cat meat, and those who do can face fines of up to NT$5 million.
- In Greece, it is illegal to feed stray cats, and those who do can face fines of up to €30,000.
- In New Zealand, it is illegal to import or sell cat fur products, and those who do can face fines of up to $100,000 NZD.

CRAZY CAT PRODUCTS THAT FAILED

- ❖ The Cat Translator promised to translate a cat's meows into human language, but it was largely ineffective and did not accurately interpret a cat's communication.

- ❖ The Cat Hammock promised to provide cats with a comfortable and elevated place to rest, but it was often difficult to install and did not support the weight of larger cats.

- ❖ The Cat Sack was a product that promised to make it easier to bathe and groom cats, but it was essentially just a bag that cats were placed in, causing discomfort and resistance.

- ❖ The Cat Lick Pad claimed to make it easier to administer medication to cats by allowing them to lick the medication off the pad, but it was largely ineffective and not well-received by cats.

- ❖ The Cat Toilet Training System promised to teach cats how to use a human toilet instead of a litter box, but it proved to be difficult to use and often resulted in unsanitary situations.

- ❖ The Catnip Spray claimed to attract cats to a certain area or object, but it was largely ineffective and did not have the same effect as traditional catnip.

- ❖ The Catnip Bubble Machine promised to provide cats with endless entertainment by blowing catnip-infused bubbles, but it was largely ineffective and did not capture the interest of most cats.

- The Catnip Plant claimed to allow cat owners to grow their own catnip, but it was difficult to grow and often did not produce the desired results.
- The Cat Music Album claimed to provide cats with relaxing music, but it was largely ineffective and did not have a noticeable effect on most cats.
- The Cat Remote Control Mouse promised to provide cats with an interactive toy that they could control, but it was largely ineffective and did not capture the interest of most cats.
- The Cat Eye Massager promised to provide cats with a soothing massage around the eye area, but it was difficult to use and often resulted in discomfort for cats.
- The Cat Water Fountain claimed to encourage cats to drink more water by providing a continuous flow of water, but it was often noisy and difficult to clean.
- The Cat Travel Bed promised to provide cats with a comfortable and secure place to rest during travel, but it was often too bulky and difficult to transport.
- The Cat GPS Tracker claimed to track a cat's location in real-time, but it was often inaccurate and unreliable.
- The Cat Selfie Stick promised to capture perfect photos of cats, but it was often difficult to use and did not produce the desired results.
- The Cat Hair Dye promised to allow owners to dye their cats' fur in various colors, but it was often harmful to cats and not well-received by the public.

AND THE CAT CAME BACK...

- Nellie the Cat was a feline who traveled more than 300 miles from her home in Massachusetts to a vacation rental in Maine, where she eventually found her way back home.
- Hamlet the Cat was a feline who traveled 373 miles from his home in Ontario to a cabin in Quebec, where he finally found his way back to his owners.
- Bailey the Cat was a feline who traveled more than 800 miles from his home in Texas to Illinois, where he finally found his way back home.

- Pudding and Tiamat were two cats who made headlines in 2019 after they walked 12 miles back to their original home after being accidentally rehomed.
- Willow the Cat was a feline who traveled more than 1,500 miles from her home in Colorado to New York City, where she finally made it back to her owners.
- Cooper the Cat was a feline who stowed away on a Canadian cargo ship and traveled more than 2,000 miles before being discovered in a container.
- Dusty the Cat was a feline who walked 3,000 miles from his home in California to a vacation rental in Wisconsin, where he was finally reunited with his owners.

PROOF THAT CATS HAVE 9 LIVES

- In 2014, a cat named Bart was hit by a car and presumed dead by his owners. Five days later, Bart showed up in a neighbor's yard, severely injured but still alive. He underwent surgery to repair his jaw and eye socket and made a full recovery.
- A cat named Andy survived a 16-story fall from an apartment building in Boston in 2012. Despite suffering from a collapsed lung, broken leg, and fractured ribs, Andy made a full recovery.

- In 2013, a cat named Lucky fell from a 26th-floor balcony in New York City and survived. Lucky suffered only minor injuries, including a fractured paw and a chipped tooth.
- In 2019, a cat named Fluffy survived being buried under a snowdrift in Montana for over an hour. Despite being covered in snow and ice and suffering from hypothermia, Fluffy made a full recovery.
- In 2007, a cat named Muffin survived being trapped in a washing machine for a full cycle. Despite suffering from hypothermia and bruises, Muffin made a full recovery.
- A cat named Kuli survived a shark attack in Hawaii in 2016. Kuli suffered injuries to his paw and tail but made a full recovery and continues to live with his owner, who is a surfer.
- In 2015, a cat named Bella survived a 20-mile ride on the engine block of a car. Despite suffering from burns and bruises, Bella made a full recovery.
- A cat named Sugar survived being hit by a car and stuck in the grille for a 19-mile drive in Florida in 2019. Despite suffering from bruises and a concussion, Sugar made a full recovery.
- In 2016, a cat named Buddy survived being trapped in a tree for five days in California. Despite suffering from dehydration and hunger, Buddy made a full recovery.
- A cat named Gin survived being accidentally trapped in a box and shipped from France to England in 2011. Despite being trapped without food or water for several days, Gin made a full recovery.
- A cat named Betty survived a 30-minute cycle in a tumble dryer in 2020. Despite suffering from burns and a broken tooth, Betty made a full recovery.
- In 2018, a cat named Miss Rigby survived a 2,500-mile journey from California to Hawaii in a shipping container. Despite being trapped without food or water for several days, Miss Rigby made a full recovery.
- A cat named Angel survived being trapped in a wall for five days in 2015. Despite suffering from dehydration and hunger, Angel made a full recovery.
- In 2016, a cat named Jasper survived being shot with an arrow in the UK. Despite suffering from injuries to his liver and stomach, Jasper made a full recovery.

- In 2017, a cat named Fluffy survived being stranded on a frozen ledge for nine days in Montana. Despite suffering from frostbite and dehydration, Fluffy made a full recovery.
- In 2020, a cat named Benji survived being hit by a train and getting stuck in the front of the locomotive in Scotland. Despite suffering from a broken jaw and other injuries, Benji made a full recovery.
- A cat named Felix survived being washed out to sea on a dinghy in 2019. Despite being stranded on an uninhabited island for several days, Felix was eventually found and rescued.

CATS UNDERSTAND MORE THAN WE THINK

- In 2020, a cat named Smudge was recorded using a computer mouse to play a video game, showing an ability to manipulate technology.
- A cat named Folsom was recorded using a stick to fish treats out of a jar in 2017, showing an understanding of tool use.
- In 2018, a cat named Pogo was recorded solving a puzzle box to retrieve treats, demonstrating problem-solving abilities.
- A cat named Rascal became famous for using a toilet brush to scratch his back in 2019, showing an ability to adapt tools for different purposes.
- In 2016, a cat named Misha was recorded using a door handle to open a door and gain access to a room.

- A cat named Eddie became famous for using a paw to turn on a faucet and drink from the sink in 2017, showing an understanding of cause-and-effect.
- A cat named Mittens became known for using a paintbrush to create art in 2019, showing an ability to use tools creatively.
- In 2018, a cat named Mango was recorded using a lever to open a window and gain access to the outdoors.
- In 2017, a cat named Zara was recorded using a plastic container to catch and carry water from a dripping faucet, showing an understanding of fluid dynamics.
- A cat named Felix became famous for using a paw to turn off an alarm clock in 2016, demonstrating an understanding of cause-and-effect.
- In 2018, a cat named Luna was recorded using a door stopper to keep a door open, demonstrating an ability to use tools creatively.

TRADITIONAL CAT LIMERICKS

- There once was a cat from Nantucket,
  Whose fur was as soft as a bucket;
  She'd curl up and purr,
  And never once stir,
  Until her owner was ready to pluck it.

- There was an old cat with a hat,
  Who sat in the sun like a mat.
  He'd yawn and he'd stretch,
  And his owners felt blessed,
  To have such a cool and calm cat.

- There was a sleek black cat named Jack,
  Whose fur was as dark as a midnight snack.
  He'd roam through the streets,
  With soft, silent feet,
  And his owners would wait up for his comeback.

- There was a mischievous cat named Mittens,
  Who would always be up to her old tricks;
  She'd climb up a tree,
  And scratch at a bee,
  And then take a nap on a pile of bricks.

- There once was a cat with a hat,
  Whose meows sounded like a rat.
  But when he was fed,
  He'd purr and he'd spread,
  Happiness to his owners, who loved him like that.

- There was a sly cat named Whiskers,
  Whose fur was like a thousand wispy whispers.
  He'd sit on his owners' lap,
  And take a long, leisurely nap,
  And they'd stroke him until they were dizzy with pleasure.

- There once was a cat with bright eyes,
  Whose presence was as smooth as pies.
  She'd rub up against,
  Her owner's leg, dense,
  And he'd pet her until she let out contented sighs.

- There was a wise cat named Socrates,
  Whose fur was as white as a breeze;
  He'd purr and he'd play,
  And never would stray,
  From his life of luxury and ease.

- There was a small cat with a face,
  Whose whiskers made her look full of grace.
  She'd sit by the window,

And stare out in limbo,
And her owners knew she was in her rightful place.

- ❖ There once was a cat with a tail,
  Whose meows sounded like a whale.
  But when he saw mice,
  He'd pounce in a trice,
  And his owners would cheer and hail.

- ❖ There was a sleek cat named Shadow,
  Whose eyes were as bright as the meadow.
  She'd run and she'd play,
  All throughout the day,
  And her owners would follow wherever she'd go.

- ❖ There was a small kitten named Tom,
  Whose meows sounded like a tiny bomb.
  He'd chase after strings,
  And other small things,
  And his owners would watch him with awe and aplomb.

- ❖ There once was a cat with nine lives,
  Whose adventures were as wild as the tides.
  He'd climb up a tree,
  Or chase after a bee,
  And his owners knew he'd always survive.

- ❖ There once was a cat from Japan,
  Whose fur was as soft as a fan;
  She'd sit and she'd stare,
  With a regal air,
  And her owners would bow like a man.

- ❖ There once was a curious cat
  Who sat on the shelf like a hat
  He pawed at the pages
  Through the long and short stages
  And dozed off at the end with a splat!

MORE RANDOM FACTS THAT DIDN'T MAKE THE CUT, BUT CAN STILL MAKE YOU SMILE...

- Certain cats go crazy for foods you wouldn't expect, like olives, potato chips, and the hops in beer.
- Cats like to sleep on things that smell like their owners, such as their pillows and dirty laundry (ick!).
- Cats love to sleep in laundry baskets, too, because they're basically hiding places with peep holes.
- For some reason, cats really dislike citrus scents. And some cats love the smell of chlorine. Go figure.
- Many cats like to lick their owner's freshly washed hair.
- Thieving behavior is not uncommon among cats. They will often grab objects like stuffed animals, feather dusters, and other things that remind them of prey.
- It turns out that Abraham Lincoln was a crazy cat president! He had four cats that lived in the White House with him.
- President Bill Clinton's cat, Socks, was a media darling during the Clinton administration and was said to receive more letters than the President himself.
- A cat's learning style is about the same as a 2- to 3-year-old child.
- A cat's purr vibrates at a frequency of 25 to 150 hertz, which is the same frequency at which muscles and bones repair themselves.
- A group of kittens is called a "kindle."
- Cats have contributed to the extinction of 33 different species.

- Cats Don't Think You're Capable Of Taking Care Of Yourself. It's why they bring you mice and other dead animals (or in the case of my two very indoor cats, toys) — they think you suck at hunting, so they're bringing you dinner. How sweet.

- The world's longest cat was a Maine Coon called Stewie, and was measured at 48.5 inches. Whereas, the record for the tallest cat belonged to Arcturus at a whopping 19.05 inches tall! Those are some big cats.

- According to Ancient History Encyclopedia, Herodotus wrote in 440BC that when a pet cat died in Ancient Egyptian times the family members would shave off their eyebrows in mourning. Now that's an interesting cat fact!

- The oldest cat to have ever lived was 38 years and 3 days old when he passed away. Creme Puff, born on 3rd August 1967 lived until 6th August 2005, and his owner Jake Perry also owned the previous oldest cat record holder, Grandpa Rex Allen, who passed away at the grand age of 34! Whatever Jake Perry's doing, he's doing it right!

- The record for the loudest purr is 67.8db. Merlin, a black and white cat from Torquay, UK, currently holds the record for the loudest purr by a domestic cat. His purr is 67.8db(A) and for context, this is nearly the same volume as a shower! Most cats purr at around 25db.

- Cats have a total of 32 muscles in each of their ears, alone! This allows them to swivel their ears to hone in on an exact noise. All these muscles help cats rotate their ears 180 degrees!

- Whether your Siamese kitten prints turn blond or brown in color is dependent on their body temperature. The Siamese cat carries albino genes which work at a body temperature of 36 Degrees Celsius.

- There is a tower in Scotland which has been built in commemoration of a cat named Towser. The tower is a celebration of all the mice she killed in her lifetime, which is a number over 30,000.

- When cats climb a tree, they can't go back down it head first. This is because their claws are facing the same way, instead, they have to go back down backward.

- A group of cats is called a "clowder."

- According to a Hebrew legend, God created cats after Noah prayed for help in protecting the food stores on the Ark from being eaten by rats. In return, God made a lion sneeze and out came a pair of cats.

- Your cat not only rubs their head against you as a sign of affection, but they are also making you as their territory. They use the scent glands they have around their face, the base of their tails, and their paws to do so.
- Cats are actually more popular in the United States than dogs are. There are around 88 million pet cats versus 75 million pet dogs.
- In Japan, cats are thought to have the power to turn into super spirits when they die. This may stem from the Buddhist believe that cats are temporary resting places for powerful and very spiritual people.
- Europe introduced cats into the Americas as a form of pest control in the 1750s.
- There are up to 70 million feral cats in the United States alone.
- In Holland's embassy in Moscow, Russia, the staff noticed that the two Siamese cats kept meowing and clawing at the walls of the building. Their owners finally investigated, thinking they would find mice. Instead, they discovered microphones hidden by Russian spies. The cats heard the microphones when they turned on. Instead of alerting the Russians that they found said microphones, they simply staged conversations about delays in work orders and suddenly problems were fixed much quicker!
- Some Evidence suggests that domesticated cats have been around since 3600 B.C.E., over 2,000 years before the Ancient Egyptians.
- Cats can recognize your voice. So yes, they are just ignoring you.
- When a family cat died in ancient Egypt, family members would shave off their eyebrows as a sign of mourning.
- Cats can move both ears separately and about 180 degrees around.
- While cats are seen as having a lower social IQ then dogs, they can solve much more difficult cognitive problems. When they feel like it of course.
- Abraham Lincoln kept three cats in the white house. After the civil war was over, Lincoln found 3 kittens whose mother had died and took them in as his own.
- Cat's, as well as other animals' noses, have their own unique print, much like a humans fingerprint.
- In just 10 years one female cat and her offspring could produce around 49,000 kittens!

- Cats spend nearly 1/3rd of their lives cleaning themselves. They also spend nearly 1/3rd of their lives sleeping.
- A Cat's spine is so flexible because it's made up of 53 loosely fitting vertebrae. Humans only have 34.
- When cats walk their back paws step almost exactly in the same place as the front paws did beforehand, this keeps noise to a minimum and limits visible tracks.
- Approximately 200 feral cats roam the grounds of Disneyland, where they help control the amusement park's rodent population. They're all spayed or neutered, and park staffers provide them with medical care and extra food.
- The Hungarian word for "quotation marks," macskaköröm, literally translates to "cat claws."
- Cats can drink seawater! Their kidneys are able to filter salt out of water, something humans can't do.
- Cats have both short term and long term memory. This means that they can remember, short term, up to 16 hours ago. Yet they tend to be more selective compared to dogs. Meaning they only remember what is beneficial to them.
- There are 473 taste buds on a cat's tongue!
- Cats and humans have nearly identical sections of the brain that control emotions.
- Cat rental services are becoming increasingly popular, especially in cities where people live in small apartments and cannot have pets of their own. They typically provide customers with a selection of cats to choose from, and customers can rent the cats for a set period of time, such as an hour or a day.
- The Cat Sìth, a mythical Scottish cat, was believed to have the ability to steal souls and control the weather, making it a mysterious and feared creature in folklore.
- The Cat Demon of Dartmoor, a legendary cat-like creature, is said to roam the moors of Dartmoor in England and is rumored to be responsible for the disappearances of numerous livestock, adding to the area's mysterious reputation.

THE END... OR IS IT?

Hey, fellow trivia addicts... Did you get your fix with "Interesting Facts for Curious Cats?" Of course, you did! But don't keep that awesomeness to yourself — let the world know by leaving a review on Amazon!

As a thank you, we've got a special gift waiting for you, absolutely free! So, what are you waiting for? Sign up now and claim your brain-boosting kitty bonus pack! Just go to:

hhfpress.com/cat

But that's not all, folks! We've got a whole library of mind-blowing trivia books to satisfy your curiosity cravings!

So, come on down and join the trivia party! Leave us a review, grab your free gift, and dive into our other fantastic books today!

Printed in Great Britain
by Amazon